THE SOCIAL CHALLENGE

THE SOCIAL CHALLENGE

Six lectures held in Zurich between 3 February and 8 March 1919

TRANSLATED BY CHRISTIANA BRYAN

INTRODUCTION BY WILLIAM FORWARD

RUDOLF STEINER

RUDOLF STEINER PRESS

CW 328

Rudolf Steiner Press
Hillside House, The Square
Forest Row, RH18 5ES

www.rudolfsteinerpress.com

Published by Rudolf Steiner Press 2025

Originally published in German under the title *Die soziale Frage* (volume 328 in the *Rudolf Steiner Gesamtausgabe* or Collected Works) by Rudolf Steiner Verlag, Dornach. Based on shorthand notes that were not reviewed or revised by the speaker. This authorized translation is based on the first German edition (1977), edited by Paul G. Bellmann und Walter Kugler

Published by permission of the Rudolf Steiner Nachlassverwaltung, Dornach

A catalogue record for this book is available from the British Library

ISBN 978 1 85584 677 7

Cover by Morgan Creative
Typeset by Symbiosys Technologies, Visakhapatnam, India
Printed and bound by 4Edge Ltd., Essex

Contents

Publisher's Note

In addition to the self-contained lecture cycle—held by Rudolf Steiner between 3 and 12 February 1919 in the main hall of the Hirschengraben School in Zurich on the subject of 'The Social Challenge'—the present volume contains two further lectures. In the first of these, also on a stand-alone topic, Steiner was speaking to Zurich students, while in the second lecture—that of 8 March, in the great hall of the Zurich Volkshaus—he was largely addressing workers.

The first of these lecture cycles formed the basis for Rudolf Steiner's essay 'Key Points of the Social Challenge—Present and Future Life Needs' (CW 23, *Towards Social Renewal*). Roman Bos, who was in the audience of these lectures and a leading light in the movement for Social Threefolding, wrote in this connection in *Sozialwissenschaftlichen Texten* ('Social Science Texts'), (Dornach 1935, 2nd edition Freiburg 1961):

> The lecture of 3 February basically appears as the first chapter of 'Key Points'. Yet what was offered was a slightly different train of thought comprising a sequence of reflections around the idea of class consciousness. (2nd edition, p.64). While the second lecture, that of 5 February, largely encompasses the contents of Chapter 2 of 'Key Points', Chapter 3, the third Zurich lecture of 10 February, is 'almost totally conceived afresh'. This treats largely of the governance and circulation of capital within a threefold social organism, whereas the lecture responding to the topic set by the audience was that of addressing threefolding once again, now from a new perspective, as the central impetus of social evolution (p.67). The content of the fourth Zurich lecture of 12 February 1919 is, in almost every detail, worked into the 3rd and 4th chapters of 'Key Points' (p.73).

These notebook entries, as well as the conceptual outline for the lecture of 8 March, provide additional insights into Rudolf Steiner's working methods. They had already appeared in part in *Nachrichten der Rudolf Steiner-Nachlaßverwaltung* ('News from Rudolf Steiner's Estate'). See in this regard the special edition *50 Jahre 'Die Kernpunkte der sozialen Frage', April 1919–April 1969* ('50 Years of Key Points of the Social Question: April 1919–April 1969'), Nos. 24/25, Dornach, Easter 1969, pp. 47–54 and No. 11, Dornach, Christmas 1963, pp. 16 and 17.

Translator's note:

Throughout this volume the terms spiritual, intellectual, academic and cultural have been used interchangeably and in varied combination depending on context. Throughout Rudolf Steiner uses the terms proletarian and proletariat and this has largely been replicated for reasons of historical accuracy. 'Workers' and 'blue collar' have occasionally been substituted.

Introduction

THERE are books that arrive like messengers—quiet, unassuming, yet bearing truths that stir something deep within us. *The Social Challenge*, newly translated, and published for the first time in English, is one such volume. It gathers six lectures Rudolf Steiner delivered in Zurich between February and March of 1919, a time when Europe stood at the threshold of profound transformation. The war had ended, but the soul of society remained fractured. Steiner did not speak into this void with slogans or systems. He spoke with the voice of someone who has been listening to those who 'cherish the hope among themselves and in others that opportunities might present themselves to counteract the anguish being so terribly visited upon humanity'.

To read these lectures is to encounter a thinker who understood that the social question is not merely economic or political—it is spiritual. Steiner's voice is not that of a reformer in the conventional sense. He does not offer a programme to be implemented, but a perception to be cultivated. He invites us to see the social organism as a living whole, composed of three distinct yet interdependent spheres: spiritual-cultural life, rights life, and economic life. Each, he insists, must be governed by its own principle—freedom, equality, and brotherhood—not as ideals, but as functional realities.

The Zurich lectures unfold like a conversation with the future. Steiner begins by diagnosing the spiritual emptiness at the heart of modern social unrest. He sees the workers' struggle not only in terms of wages and conditions, but as a cry for meaning—a longing to reconnect with the cultural and spiritual life from which they have been excluded. This insight alone sets Steiner apart from the ideologues of his time. He does not dismiss the proletarian movement;

he listens to it, and hears in its depths a call for renewal. 'Unlike perhaps any other movement in the world, the contemporary workers' movement is one that has sprung from thinking. ... For years I worked in a workers' college, giving classes to working people from the most varied branches of industry. I became familiar with what animates workers' psyches and motivates them. From this vantage point I learnt much about live issues among trades unions of various occupations and professions. In other words, what I say are not just theoretical musings or apercus but the result of real life experience.'

As the lectures progress, Steiner introduces the architecture of the threefold social organism. He is careful not to impose a rigid structure. Instead, he speaks of organic differentiation—of allowing each sphere to evolve according to its own nature. Spiritual life must be free from state control. Legal life must be grounded in equality before the law. Economic life must be shaped by cooperation and mutual responsibility. These are not abstractions. They are principles that arise from a deep understanding of human nature and social reality.

Steiner's critique of ideology is especially poignant. He warns against fanaticism—against the temptation to reduce complex human realities to simplistic formulas. He sees Marxist materialism not as evil, but as incomplete. It lacks the spiritual dimension without which no true social renewal is possible. Steiner's call is for real social thinking—thinking that arises from life itself, from people engaging with each other in any given situation—not from dogma.

Throughout the lectures, Steiner returns again and again to the theme of inner development. He insists that outer reform must be grounded in inner transformation. The social will, he says, must be nourished by spiritual insight. Only a threefold social order can free labour from commodification. This is perhaps the most challenging aspect of Steiner's vision. It asks us not only to change society, but to change ourselves, and it is realistic enough to see that this will not happen quickly—although step changes in human development, he insists, are possible.

The final lecture, delivered on 8 March, 1919, is a quiet crescendo. Taking us through each of the constituent parts of the social order in turn, he outlines the steps toward renewal—not as a blueprint, but as a living impulse. He speaks of civic courage, of spiritual education, of economic brotherhood. He does not promise utopia. He offers a path 'which really has to escalate into becoming a vast world-historic transformation which will progress from present proletarian consciousness, advancing to become universal human consciousness. What others have hitherto been unable to establish will then, founded in the dignity of contemporary proletarians, be established as true human dignity for all humankind'.

This volume is not light reading. Nor should it be. It is a companion for those who sense that the social question is, at heart, a spiritual question.

In our own time, when society once again trembles at the edge of transformation, Steiner's voice speaks with renewed relevance. He does not tell us what to do. He asks us to listen—to the world, to one another, and to the quiet stirrings of conscience. *The Social Challenge* is not a solution. It is a seed. And those who read it with care may find themselves called to cultivate something new.

William Forward
September 2025

Lecture 1

Zurich, 3 February 1919

The true dimensions of the social challenge, based on spiritual-scientific research into human needs

What is entailed in the social challenge has been of intense concern to thoughtful humanity over recent decades. Concern because not only can this challenge be said to be crucial for humanity's onward evolution but because it has become something of a burning issue. The horrific catastrophe of war, in particular, has broken over humanity in recent years and has thrown a bleak spotlight onto these societal issues and their associated pan-human movements.

Because I need to place the historic conundrum of society at the centre of recent times, I will over the course of coming lectures have to address various issues connected with the cause and course of that hideously disastrous war. In these introductory remarks I would just like to mention how—right from the outset of war—social questions were jostling among feelings of fear clearly discernible among those at the source of hostilities. Much would undoubtedly have gone differently in 1914 had decision makers not been operating under such fear as to what might transpire were social movements increasingly to assert themselves. Much of what has resulted from this so-called war came about due, on the one hand, to fear and, on the other, to a number of leading figures totally misconstruing social imperatives. Much would have turned out differently had fear and misunderstanding not been so prevalent. And yet we see how, over the course of the war, people active within the social movement cherish the hope among themselves and in others that opportunities might present themselves to counteract the anguish being so terribly visited upon humanity. Now that these tragic events have reached a certain crisis point, we see that, especially in defeated countries, these residual upshots persist: the most desperate need to take a stand on social issues and to intercede on behalf of present social needs.

On this basis alone, anyone surveying and reflecting on the present—anyone with the slightest inclination to inform themselves about present conditions—will see that what is emerging amid social life will concern every member of society for a very, very long time. At this moment when, as I said, subjugated countries need every effort to solve their social woes, something akin to tragedy has settled over vast swathes of the developed world.

If you survey spiritual-intellectual achievements, literature and related areas that have arisen from discussion, colloquia and efforts devoted to social issues, an immeasurable amount of work and thinking are involved. Yet never have we faced social problems of such urgency as now. Today, life itself shows us the scale of social challenges. Despite every endeavour, every effort of thinking and the best will in the world, it appears as though anything of consequence, any capabilities developed over past decades, have turned out to be totally inadequate in dealing with social issues when presented in their true form, that is, as wrought by life itself. This bears down oppressively onto present efforts as an immense tragedy. Something so long in preparation and involving precisely those people whom one would have liked to believe were crucial are seemingly quite unprepared.

Anyone genuinely grappling with social questions over these past decades—not just those acting from a perspective of theoretical science, dry abstraction or unilateral partiality—will have found that powerfully paradoxical inconsistencies have always cropped up in this area. Perhaps the following is one of the most striking of these social disparities to emerge. Much could be heard of discussions, much could be gleaned from written material by people placed by life in the contemporary social movement. Particularly from those at the centre of discussions, from those attuned to the will of a modern workforce, you could sense that, yes indeed, all sorts of issues were being mooted, all sorts of topics raised, including questions asked about life's vital dynamics while attempts are being made to give direction to various initiatives. But within what we can call social will or willing lies something quite, quite different from what is being articulated. Faced with hardly any other phenomenon in life can the feeling be so clearly sensed that largely subconscious, unspoken elements are playing a greater part than what is being expressed in seemingly clear concepts and finding its way into sober discussion. This is the point at which you can find cause not to despair of attempts being made to tackle social problems, albeit from a specific perspective.

Here in Zurich, as in other Swiss cities, I have often been invited to speak about aspects of spiritual science. From a perspective of spiritual-scientific research, I have for decades sought to focus on the social conundrum. Today, hearing those deeming themselves to be practical people, you might well despair of anything constructive being contributed from a perspective of academic research. Yet the very contradictory nature of social life—this needs to be emphasized—will again dispel any such despair. You see how leading figures in the social movement smile when talk turns to some spiritually-aligned attempt or other aimed at resolving social problems. They deride this as ideology and questionable theory. They don't think that something based purely in thinking or spiritual sources will be capable of contributing usefully to today's burning issues. But if you look more closely, the thought occurs forcibly that the root nerve, the very underlying impetus of the modern working-class movement, lies not in what its members are talking about but rather in *thinking*.

Unlike perhaps any other movement in the world, the contemporary workers' movement is one that has sprung from *thinking*, and on closer inspection this is patently apparent. I say this not just as a clever aside or aperçu. If I may be permitted a personal remark here. For years I worked in a workers' college, giving classes to working people from the most varied branches of industry. I became familiar with what animates workers' psyches and motivates them. From this vantage point I learnt much about live issues among trades unions of various occupations and professions. In other words, what I say are not just theoretical musings or aperçus but the result of real-life experience.[1]

Those who are familiar with the contemporary workers' movement on the ground—and this is unfortunately rarely the case among leading intellectuals—where it is actually set up by working people themselves, will know what a wonderful phenomenon this is. How a particular direction in thinking—a remarkable stream of thought—has gripped and inspired these people in the most intensive ways. This is what makes it so difficult nowadays to take a position on societal enigmas and means that such meagre prospects for mutual understanding exist between classes. The middle classes find it very difficult to put themselves into the shoes of blue-collar workers and have such a problem understanding what I would like to call their uncorrupted intelligence, in which an elemental force, an intellectual challenge such as that found in the thought system of Karl Marx[2] can take hold—regardless of how you may relate to its contents.

Undoubtedly, Karl Marx's thought system is acceptable to some, rejected by others, for reasons perhaps as sound for one group as for the other. It could be highly regarded by those who continued to view societal life in the manner of Marx and his friend Engels[3] after their deaths. I do not wish to comment on the content of this system, of this scheme of thought—it is of minimal interest, it seems to me. What strikes me as significant is this fact: within workforces, within proletarianism, the most powerful force at work is a system of thought. This can be expressed as follows. No other practical movement, no solely life-based movement espousing the most everyday of human demands has ever existed in such near-total isolation on a purely scientific, ideological basis as this workers' movement. It is even in some respects the first such movement in the world to be founded on purely scientific bases. And yet—as I hinted earlier—if, on closer observation of life itself, you take all that the contemporary worker has to say about their own opinions, will and feelings, this turns out not to be the crucial factor.

Many have demonstrated most astutely how this working-class social movement arose from the evolution of the last centuries. It has been cleverly elaborated how proletarianism—particularly on account of developments in technology and mechanical advances—

came about in its present form in the first place; how, due to the enormously fluctuating economic tides of recent times, any social query at all arose. I will not repeat here what others have so ingeniously expounded about the rise of societal issues. But it seems to me necessary to point in particular to what characterizes the inequities—the real-life inconsistencies—in this workers' movement. It is true that this movement could not have come about without the recent gigantic upheavals and turmoil of the technical revolution and the form in which it has evolved. However heatedly it is claimed that what is now manifesting in social life is solely a result of commercial pressures or economic forces, class differences and class warfare, when you observe working life in more detail and at deeper levels, the claim that only economic disparities and forces play a role here does not stack up. It is precisely to those in the habit of looking more closely, spiritual-scientifically, at the subtleties and nature of human soul life—something about which even the bearer of that soul may not be conscious—that it is most obvious that the advances in technology and commerce are not the determining factors in today's social challenges. Instead, the pivotal fact is that some people have been removed from quite different circumstances and consigned to the service of machinery due to the way in which big business is run; and that, through this trans- or dislocation, an element has been activated in them that is not directly connected with their economic environment but which entails them being economically ensnared. What has been activated is linked with recent humanity's deepest habits.

Those who regard history exclusively in the way socialist science likes to do—continually reiterating the obstinately dry link between cause and effect—take no account of forces for change and transformation present in lived reality, which can at given points have revolutionary effects on that history.

Let's look at the development of an individual human being. We can follow this in successive stages from birth to around age seven and the change of dentition. Here the developing human organism undergoes a mighty revolution.[4] You have to focus on what actually takes place: it is not a simple linear progression of cause and effect. From seven to approaching fourteen or fifteen, however, a linear sequence of cause and effect is indeed apparent. Then another revolutionary moment occurs in the body when sexual maturity is reached. Later such transformative points are less obvious, but do nevertheless exist. Just as in individual lives radical moments occur, giving the lie to the endlessly repeated but false refrain that nature never makes leaps, so likewise in the historical evolution of humanity. Colossal transformations have been playing out since around the fourteenth to fifteenth centuries into the present—and will continue to do so in the future—involving processes of change in consciousness itself.

Just as the human organism differs in some respects from its earlier condition once it is sexually mature, the social organism is similarly transformed once the basic underlying impetus—not merely linear in the sense of cause and effect—has made manifest its effects. Those able to observe history accurately are aware that, before the advent of the present age, much of an instinctive nature was at work which is emerging into awareness and which must now be grasped in full consciousness. That is why the social movement is now—at a time rather typical of it—assuming a form and emerging under a much-used label, a descriptor not as intensely descriptive as it ought to be: proletarian class consciousness. As regards the term 'proletarian class consciousness': you should take less notice of it being essentially indicative of warfare—something in which proletarians mire themselves, believing themselves to be at war with the other classes—than noticing that an element has come into proletarian awareness just when the social *instincts* of times gone by are being transformed into social *consciousness*. Once there were social instincts. Now what underlies the social movement is class consciousness.

This class consciousness, I should say, only applies superficially, if one is to take the idea of class consciousness seriously. What lies concealed behind this concept of class consciousness is something quite different. To briefly characterize a salient fact: within old professional groupings, as manifest for instance in associations or guilds of craftspeople or other trades, certain social instincts were active, radiating into human souls and fortifying them. These instincts were able to work in such a way that they created a certain personal bond between what people thought, felt and willed, what they felt essential to their honour, for their delight and aesthetic needs. Work itself provided for some of these needs.

Once human beings had been installed amongst machinery, once they had been inserted into the thoroughly impersonal business of modern capitalism, where the process through to remuneration for a manually-finished product was no longer clearly transparent, but where the main aim has become to increase capital through capital itself; in other words, once people had been installed, on the one hand, in mechanized industry, on the other, into capitalism and its economic system, they were torn from their previous working lives and contexts, which had rewarded them with something of personal value for their honour, for their joy, for their own willed initiatives. People at the zenith of their personal abilities were set alongside machinery and within the solely objective and impersonal circulation of goods and capital, things of no real personal concern to them. Yet people always long to be fully engaged, to unfold their full potential. This is how a working person, plucked out of their life's context, as described, could be transposed into a context where, detached from the full vitality of their humanness, they could be directed to ponder their human dignity and to feel in retrospect that dignity.

This is how, concealed behind what is termed proletarian class consciousness, an ascendant gleam has dawned in modern historical evolution: the advent of a consciousness created from out of the human soul itself. By diverting consciousness towards the question: What am I as a human being? and: What do I signify as a person in the world? Workers, placed among humanity-negating machinery and capitalism, had occasion to ponder questions of this kind.

Yet I believe that the entire study of societal issues is put onto a different footing if you consider that, although other people, largely as a result of life circumstances that did not produce such revolutionary ferment, have been removed from their old instinctual parameters and driven towards modern consciousness, today's workers have been radically propelled into conscious self-perception away from what was formerly an instinctive understanding of human dignity and the place of the individual in society.

Now, this consciousness of humanity dawned among proletarians together with much else taking place in human progress. It coincided with a specific phase in evolution and thinking. Today, humanity's historical evolution is very poorly understood because various factions portray it in biased, partisan ways. If you look at human evolution impartially, quite different features often emerge from those traditionally discussed. It can also be said that anyone seeing what enjoys the most powerful authority these days—that is, science—knows that even what is now broadly endowed with absolute objectivity clearly bears the hallmarks of having evolved out of something preceding it and will again take on different forms in future. If you look at science with its shiny methods, its endlessly conscientious research techniques, at the science so well suited to penetrating nature's manifest phenomena, you notice that the most perceptive thing it can express is that, basically, it is ill-equipped to grasp the deepest inward human feeling and intuiting, that it has precious little to say about what people want to know when turning their attention to self-knowledge and conceptions of themselves. Science has also in some respects severed itself from the human being. It no longer bears personal features nor does it speak of any spiritual, supra-sensible or eternal element in the human being. If it mentions any of these at all, it makes fashionably clear that it possesses no corresponding methodology nor compatible research tools.

You can look back from this form of science to times in human evolution when life was fully embedded in a religious conception of the world, in religious sentience and scientific observing. These moved apart. What had been unified diverged at around the same time as the revolution in objectivity that found expression in the machine age when the emergence of capitalism was taking place. While this economic cataclysm was in process, it was as if religious growth largely wished to stand still, did not want to participate in, nor accompany, all that stemmed from scientific development. Then, at a time when such as Galileo and Giordano Bruno were being condemned,[5] those most inward human feelings and sensitivities remained, in one sense, behind in the face of what people would voluntarily say about nature and the world. People lost their belief that they could still suffuse their knowledge with a religious glow, with any religious warmth. Nowadays people are immensely proud that science can be maintained free of elements they wish to ascribe to religion alone. It is into this timeframe, when science is increasingly aiming to be totally religion- and spirit-free, that proletarians' evolving consciousness and dawning pan-human awareness falls.

The proletariat forged ahead to modern thinking, to modern intelligence, to a grasp of what can be understood through force of spiritual intellect. It encountered a science which no longer contained the momentum to encompass and fulfil human beings in their entirety. And it is this that has given the modern proletarian psyche its distinctive configuration. Humanity's spiritual consciousness, spiritual awareness among leading classes, as it had been in times gone by, had also lost its momentum, had delivered a science that was largely remote and abstracted from human conditions. This is what proletarians experienced at a soul level when faced with a science that could inspire no trust that it could provide the most truthful, inward spirit reality amid external sense- and economic activity. This is the science they saw they faced and for which they had to settle. This is how something entered their psyches from purely spiritual-evolutionary substrata, something which today manifests as a sort of irrefutable certainty, accepted as absolute truth, whose true nature is only identifiable in terms of soul processes. What moves the closer observer most is the way in which workers will speak about actual issues of spirit, convention, morality, art, religion, evolution, even of science, incorporating all this under a heading of *ideology*. This is very moving, and never more so than when you see how sure they believe themselves to be that everything humans think, all that they create artistically, all religious feeling, is just a soul-generated simulacrum, is just ideology. However, it is economic struggle and commercial processes that constitute real actuality for them. Humankind's spiritual evolution is pitched into their soul mix as a sort of reflected gleam. It is ideology. At best it deflects a few impulses back into the purely material reality of economic proceedings. Rebounding into economic practices, this view is itself a product of those self-same economic processes.

This position on spirituality exists in proletarianism as something far more fundamental than one might think. Why, oh why, have art, tradition, morality, religion and sundry other intangible spiritual attributes become ideology for modern working people? Because they have inherited from previously leading echelons a science that no longer wants to support a living connection with the genuine world of spirit, a science that shows not the slightest impetus towards real spirituality. Science of this sort is at best capable of leading to abstract concepts in the form of natural laws. It can lead nowhere else than to a view of spirituality as an ideology. It yields methodologies suited, on the one hand, to purely objective, non-human nature and, within human life on the other, to economic proceedings. When proletarians were obliged to take on this scientific bias, their outlook became focused as if by a powerfully suggestive force on the sole area science of this sort is capable of focusing: on economic life. And they started to believe this economic existence to be their only reality, whereas in truth the science bequeathed them by bourgeois echelons *could* lead only to economic life.

Yet this was enormously pivotal because it gave the working-class movement its actual, characteristic impetus. You can see how old instinctual elements still lingered in this movement right into the last decades of the nineteenth century. You can still find in some old programmes and courses[6] points at which the concept of human dignity and the exercise of rights that result in true dignity were discussed. Since the 1890s we have been seeing—under influences just described—how proletarians' focus and that of their learned champions has been bent as if by a powerful force of suggestion solely towards the economy. Now they no longer believe that anywhere other than in an economy can a spiritual or soulful incentive exist of the kind that is so fundamental to any social movement. They believed that only via the un-spiritual, un-soulful economy could conditions they deemed worthy of humankind be achieved. So they turned their attention to transforming economic life itself so as to rid it of all the harm caused by individual employers' egotism in private enterprise, and to be shielded from the failure of those employers to honour employees' demands relating to human dignity. This is how workers started to enact the only possible means they could see of transferring private property and the means of production into communal control or even communal ownership. Underlying this—and its only outcome—is what happens when attention is diverted away from anything of a soul-spiritual nature, when spirit becomes ideology; when everything is based on quasi-scientific methodology only capable of resulting in economic considerations.

A remarkable fact now emerged, one that demonstrates just how many inconsistencies exist in the proletarian movement. The modern worker believes that the economy and all economic life ought to evolve in such a way that it ultimately embodies all their human rights. As they see it, they are fighting for full human rights. Even within this aspiration, a fact emerges which cannot possibly arise as a result of economics alone. This important fact is tellingly insistent and lies at the core of all aspects of the societal challenge, proceeding as it does from vital human imperatives. It is something they believe to have arisen from the economy itself—something it could never have been—but which is a result, rather, of the direct linear evolution from ancient slavery, via feudal times, to present-day working proletarians. In whichever form the circulation of goods and money, the essentials of capitalism, ownership, the nature of land and property ownership and so on may have developed, within modern life an element has emerged that is not clearly articulated by proletarians, yet which is all too unmistakably felt to be the actual, underlying impetus of their social will. It is like this. Basically, the modern capitalist economic system only recognizes goods, products, commodities, within its sphere of circulation. It knows how these create value within the economy. And it is within the capitalist edifice of recent times that one component has become a commodity and workers feel that it cannot be allowed to be commodified. Yet, scientifically speaking, it cannot be expressed in any other way because their focus has been directed solely towards an economy where everything is commodifiable: their own labour has become a commodity.

If only there were some measure of understanding that herein lies one of the most fundamental aspects of the entire workers' movement and that, at an instinctive and subconscious level, working people feel that selling their labour to an employer in the same way as goods are sold in the market place under conditions of supply and demand is abhorrent. They detest the role their work plays in a labour market subject to supply and demand. If only it could be understood and viewed without bias that an abhorrence of these trading terms—terms not even examined radically and incisively in socialist theory—underpin the social movement of today, the very point of origin would have been identified from which all that is so pressingly and searingly manifest in the social movement ensues.

In times gone by, slavery existed. Human beings in their entirety—perhaps slightly less than their entirety, but not far off—were sold as tradeable objects into serfdom and bondage. Capitalism has become the power which still retains the subtext that people can be claimed to be goods in the form of their labour. The means need to be sought by which human labour can be disconnected, severed from other commodities in circulation. What lies behind this fact will only be grasped once the economy has shed all implication of slavery and is understood in terms that differentiate between trade and human being. Then it will become clear how the nature of human labour originates in—and must flow from—a completely different experience of society, one devoid of commercial correlation. It is essential to see—and spiritual science will supply the foundations so to do—that it is misguided to believe that just by observing the economy—to which only natural-scientific parameters apply—a way will be found to integrate an individual's labour into the social organism. People will only be on the right track once they appreciate that believing labour to belong to the economic system is tantamount to believing heart-lung-and-circulation to be processes identical with those of head and nervous system. The nerve-sense system, centred as it is in the head, is an independent, self-sufficient entity, heart-lung-circulatory system likewise, metabolism similarly. This can be found in more detail in my book *Riddles of the Soul*.[7] It is characteristic of the human organism that its systems develop and function correctly precisely in not being centralized but in coexisting freely and functioning in parallel with each other. If today it is barely possible to think of the human body with keen synthesis, even less is it possible to understand the social organism via an unreconstructed science in dire need of spiritual-scientific reform. The human body is thought today to be a single centralized unit when in fact it is threefold in structure.

The societal organism is also threefold in structure. Viewed under great power of suggestion as a single entity, the economy is in fact just one element of society. A further element is what must ensue from an understanding of the function of human labour within the overall structure of society. Both systems have to exist alongside one another. Then labour will be defined as a commodity only in the deceptive thinking of recent times.

The tight-fisted, hard-hearted thinking of recent times has made mere ideology of the third element belonging to the social organism: spiritual-intellectual culture. The theoretical view that spiritual culture is mere ideology is the least dangerous. The most critical aspect of this is when the idea takes root that spirituality is mere ideology and that no genuine impetus can exist in the spirit underlying all manifestation. People in this mould have no interest in attributing to spiritual processes their rightful role in the world.

If you observe what constitutes life's vital needs, as played out in the arena of proletarian consciousness, you find that no insight into the three spheres of the social organism can be found. It is lost to view. There is a determination to nationalize because the belief persists that a single unitary social organism can shoulder responsibility for everything.

In these burningly intense times, spiritual science needs to open up broader horizons on the societal conundrum than those generally proffered by its appointed leaders. It needs mentioning that we ought not to want innovation for its own sake, but that we need to *think innovatively*, that we need not only a scientific view of social living—a view adopted by traditional science—but rather to establish anew a science that brings to human consciousness new thinking about society, thinking that is grounded in reality.

That has to lead to the source of so much recent adversity being remedied by consciousness of humanity as a whole. Those who do not work theoretically but on a basis of real-life experience—as I believe I, too, have been able to do throughout this hour—are likely to be dismissed and rendered innocuous primarily by those who consider themselves to be the really practical people: the ones who say: 'We know nothing productive will come of their theorizing. Those "practical lifers" are the abstractionists here, those "practical-experiencers" who restrict their senses to the narrowest tram-tracks, it is those "experientialists" who have added to the woes of these awful times. If they carry on their economic meddling, our woes will never end but grow exponentially.'

Yet people genuinely grounded in practical life, those who speak of developmental potential, those embedded in spatial and temporal societal evolution must—in parallel with individuals' evolution—maintain their due positions in public activity, as befits them. Today, genuinely practical people who speak out of a deeper reality are the very ones with whom we ought to be reckoning. They are the ones who need not despair of their experience and knowledge. They see where the trouble lies and regret that 'practical-lifers'—whether socialist or not—believe they have to single-handedly carry out what can only lead to ruthless exploitation in real life. Anyone wanting to work truly practically from out of the spirit will work towards a reality that is compatible with—and suited to—that real life.

The day after tomorrow I aim to address the extent to which attempts can succeed in resolving the questions I have sought to raise in their true form—based as they are on research into the social realities of habitual modes of living, and how humanity's social structures can be transformed.

Lecture 2

Zurich, 5 February 1919

Attempts at solving social issues from a spiritual-scientific perspective aligned with life and congruent with reality

A propos the themes I am developing, I would like to express the plea that you regard these four lectures as an integrated whole, so that what is presented in any one lecture is not taken in isolation and judged out of context. The subject under consideration is so extensive that it can only be tackled over the course of several lectures.

In today's lecture I would initially like to speak in sketch form about such attempts at resolution as are based on genuine knowledge of the social organism's nature, such attempts at solving social issues as *do not* originate unilaterally in the demands of any one societal echelon, class, rank or position, but which proceed from suitably life-congruent studies of evolutionary forces, particularly those presently evolving and affecting the near future. If seeking to offer a solution to social problems based on the aspirations and demands of one echelon or class of society—indeed of any one sector—it cannot be otherwise than what is achieved for one sector will have consequences for other social groupings that may in some way be inimical to their progress or the welfare of their living conditions.

The truth to which I refer, and which I will substantiate over the course of these lectures, applies to all modern life—you could say to the entire social organism—which has taken on a specific configuration due to what I described as a decisive recent factor, attributable to technology and everything involved in the technical operation of the economy and the capitalist practices that govern economic life. What modern technology and capitalism have introduced into life has necessarily attracted not only keen attention to society's social structures but also largely unconscious, yet determinative, powers of instinct.

What has produced this particular social configuration can be expressed as follows. The economy, underpinned by technology and capitalism, has had an idiosyncratic effect and has conferred on modern society a definite internal configuration. In addition to the focus on what technology and capitalism have brought to humanity, attention has been deflected away from other sectors of society which need to be activated if the social organism is to become as robust as the economy.

In order to enlarge on what I believe I have identified as the central nexus of a wide-ranging, far-reaching study of the social challenge, I'd like to begin with a comparison. But I ask you to bear in mind that I intend only to make this comparison for the purpose of lending to your understanding the wherewithal to envision the healing of society. Those used to attending to the most complex of organisms—the human body—will need to focus on the fact that it is naturally dependent on three systems working alongside each other in mutual harmony. These three interdependent systems can be outlined as follows.

Firstly, a system active in the human constitution comprising nerves and senses, centralized primarily in the head.

Secondly, what I would term a rhythmic system, connected as it is with breathing, blood circulation and everything expressed in rhythmical processes.

Thirdly, a recognizable system connected with the organs and activity involved in metabolizing.

These three systems contain all that constitutes and supports health when salutogenically integrated.

In full accord with all that natural-scientific research can confirm, I aimed to outline, albeit in sketch form, this tri-partition, this threefoldness, in my book *Riddles of the Soul*. I am sure that everything biology, physiology—natural science as a whole—will imminently discover about human beings will lead to just such interpretations and conclusions as I outlined as head-nerve, rhythmic-circulatory- and metabolic systems in terms of what maintains the overall organism, how these elements are integrated with a degree of obviousness, that there is no discernible centralizing factor and that each of these systems has a distinct relationship with the external environment: the head system via the senses, the circulatory or rhythmic system through breathing and the metabolic system through nutrition and digestion.

As regards natural-scientific methods themselves, we are not yet sufficiently advanced as to enjoy widespread acceptance by science at large of what I am outlining here in a form originating in spiritual-scientific bedrock—something for which I have been trying to gain recognition because it is of advantage to wider natural-scientific progress. What is implied, however, is that our habits of thought and our entire approach to imagining the world are not yet wholly compatible with, for instance, what constitute the essential qualities of nature's effects in the human body. You could in a sense say that natural science can wait; it will hurry in pursuit of its principles and will eventually arrive at a point where it claims this method of observing as its own.

But as regards examining the workings of the social organism, this cannot wait. Even a rudimentary understanding of society must not be left to specialist authorities but ought to exist in everyone; because everyone participates in society's impacts and, at least instinctively, knows what society needs. Wholesome thinking and feeling, solid initiative of will to shape society—even if only on an instinctive level—can only develop if you are clear that for this organism to be wholesome it needs to be as threefold in structure as the human body.

I am at a point where I must guard against being misunderstood. Since Schäffle[8] wrote his book on the structure of the social entity, there have been repeated attempts to establish analogies between the way in which creatures and human beings are naturally organized in terms of their social contexts. How many and varied are the ways in which it has been attempted to define what in society constitute cells, cellular structures, networks or webs and so on! Recently, Meray[9] wrote a book entitled *World Mutation* in which he opines that certain natural-scientific facts and laws can simply be transposed onto human societies. What is intended here, today, has nothing whatsoever to do with all such fatuous talk of analogies. Anyone who, after these lectures, says: 'Aha, here we go again, analogizing between natural organisms and societal structures' will only be proving that they lack insight into the true spirit of what is intended here. Because this is what I do *not* want: that a truth passing as some natural-scientific fact or other is transposed, overlaid onto the social organism. But I *do* want your thinking and feeling to learn, by observing natural entities, that its methods, its means of sensing, can then be applied to the societal organism. If you simply transpose what you believe you have learnt about natural organisms—in the way that Schäffle's book *World Mutation* and others do—you simply demonstrate that you have no wish to acquire faculties capable of investigating society *in terms of its own inherent laws*, nor even in as impartial a way as those who study nature's creatures according to their own lights. Because the minute you start—as objectively as a natural scientist treats natural phenomena—to apply this method wholesale to a society containing its own inherent laws, all games of analogy end.

I will say straight away why this game of analogies has to stop. When observing what ought to be a healthy social organism—albeit we are dealing with evolving, even newly-occurring phenomena—those observations will lead to a threefold social structure. Yet each element has to be accepted on its own terms if you wish to be objective. On the one hand, the three elements of the human constitution can be identified, on the other, the three components of the social organism can similarly be seen in their objective, internally-lawful mutuality. Were you to seek analogies, you might proceed as follows. You might say that the human head- or nerve-sense system shares some commonality with a cultural-spiritual sphere of capacities; the circulatory system mediates the polarity between this spiritual element and the coarsest system, that is, the material system of metabolism. This metabolic system—emanating from subconscious levels—can be viewed as the least refined of human systems. What would follow on from one of these games of analogy? The next stage would be to claim that, of course, society can be divided into three segments. Spiritual culture unfolds within each person. That would be one element. In it, political life as such unfolds—we will speak later about this sphere—but within it economic life also takes place. If you wanted to play the game of analogy, you might believe that spiritual life and culture in society are subject to laws that might be compared with the intellectual nerve-sense system. The coarsest system, the metabolic system, seen as the most material in the human entelechy, would by analogy-game probably be aligned with what some call the grossly material nature of the economy and industry. Those able to look at all this less partially—and who reject games of analogy—know that it is precisely the opposite way round from simple analogies. For the social organism, what mirrors economic production, consumption and the circulation of goods are the laws that in the human body underlie the nerve-sense system: specifically spiritual laws. Admittedly, the sphere of public legislature and rights—politics as such, a sphere often too comprehensively imagined—can be compared with the rhythmic system, the regulating agency of heart-and-breathing, operating as it does between two naturally-occurring systems, those of metabolic and nerve-sense polarities. But it is *only* comparable in mediating between metabolic and nerve-sense systems. Central to the circulation-rhythmic system, as in the human being, the legislative sphere of public rights exists between economy and spiritual culture. This spiritual-intellectual cultural sphere is not subject to law and cannot be thought analogous with human talent nor the nerve-sense system but rather with that spirituality within the social organism which contains laws only comparable with laws of metabolism, that least refined area in the human body.

It is to this that objective scrutiny of the body social leads. So that no misunderstanding of these points enters the discourse, they have to be predicated upon not believing that physiological or biological comparators are simply being transposed onto social life. Social life must at all times be regarded as autonomous if it is to attract to itself all that is vital to it thriving and being restored to health.

How often is the word 'socialization' heard from various quarters of Eastern and Central Europe. This socialization will bring about no healing but will be a process of social quackery—of destruction, even—unless in to human hearts and minds there is at least an instinctive recognition of the need to organize society along threefold lines. If it is to function wholesomely, society does need to encompass these three constituent parts.

Starting firstly—we could, of course, start from the perspective of spiritual culture—let's begin with the economy because this preponderates over all other aspects of life. Having imported technology and capitalism into human existence, the economic-commercial sphere can be regarded as the first of these three elements. As we will see, in part today, in part over the course of subsequent lectures, it has to be an autonomous, self-contained sector within the social organism, just as the nerve-sense system exists in relative independence in the human totality. The economy and everything to do with the production, circulation and consumption of goods constitutes mercantile life. Everything interrelating with these three functions makes up trade or commerce. We will become more familiar with its unique features over time.

Secondly, we could regard the sphere of public rights as the next element in society, politics per se and that area hitherto involving state legislation, state life per se. Whereas an economy entails all that human beings require from nature, from their own production, trading in goods, circulating commodities and consumption thereof, this second component of societal life only involves what emanates from purely human substrata and affects relationships between human beings. I ask you to take particular note of this because it is essential for correctly grasping these societal elements that you know the differences separating this system of public rights—which for profound reasons can only affect human-to-human relations—and the economy, which only involves goods or commodities, trading circulation and consumption of its products. This needs to be understood as clearly as differentiating between lung and external air in the human body—how air is processed—and the way in which nutrients taken into the *third* natural system are transformed for human benefit.

A *third* element, to be accommodated independently alongside the other two systems distinguishable in the social organism, is everything pertaining to spiritual-intellectual culture. This might be expressed more precisely because the term 'spiritual-intellectual culture' and everything referring to spiritual activity is itself not clearly delineated. Thus: everything relying on the natural talent of human individuals which adds to societal life, enhancing it out of natural giftedness, physical and mental. Whereas the first sphere—that of the economy—has everything to do with what human beings require to organize their material bond with the wider world, and the second sphere involves all that takes place in society between human beings, a third system—for which I have used the label spiritual, because it needed a name—is concerned with all that brims and wells forth from the human individuality and has to be integrated into society.

It is as true to say that technology and capitalism have of late been putting their stamp on our lives as it is essential for the wounds they have necessarily inflicted to be healed by bringing society into rightful order—as characterized here—in the form of its three elements. The economy, due entirely to its own nature, has taken on quite distinct forms and has, as it were, forced its own inherent laws onto all human life. Both the other areas of society are in place—with the same matter-of-course justification—to become rightly integrated into the social fabric according to their own inherent laws. This requires people to take on and engage with the social organism, each in their locality. Because in terms of those attempts at resolving social issues—in the sense here intended—each individual has their own social task, now and in the near future.

The first sphere in social life—that of the economy—relies primarily upon nature and its resources. Just as the individual, evolving through learning and education over the course of their life, depends on the skills and talents with which their psyche and their physical organism are gifted—those with which they are endowed—so too does all economic activity depend on certain natural foundations. These natural foundations confer on commercial life—hence also on social life—their distinct imprint. This natural basis, however, simply exists and can be encountered in its original form, uninfluenced by any social organism or process of socialization. This has to be taken into account. Just as education has to take account of any talent, natural physical gifts or intellectual diligence its charges may possess, similarly must all socialization, every attempt to give human coexistence an economic- commercial form, take account of its natural foundations. Because, underlying all circulation of goods and human labour—as also spiritual culture of all kinds—is a primordial, elemental force that binds human beings to a particular patch of the natural world. You really have to think about the connection which exists between the social organism and its natural foundations[10] in the same way as you think about educating individuals in the context of their talents. You can elaborate on this for yourselves particularly by using extreme examples. You only have to consider certain areas of the world—in which, say, bananas are a local food source—and what is required in that social context in terms of labour to transport a product such as this from its place of origin to its destination as a consumable. If you compare the human labour involved in connecting bananas with their consumer markets—let's say, central Europe—with processing wheat into consumable products, the work required for bananas is, conservatively, some three hundred times less. Labour input into wheat products is therefore some three hundred times higher.

This is certainly an extreme case. Yet such differentials in terms of labour requirements in relation to naturally-occurring resources also exist between our various branches of productive industry as they exist in one European country or another. They may not be such radical differences as between bananas and wheat products, but they do exist. So, all trade is fundamentally based—through relations between human beings, their consumption of natural resources and the extent of available labour—on nature. In a similar way, the essential being of a person depends on their natural physical condition and spiritual-intellectual gifts. You need only compare the following: in Germany, in areas with average productivity, wheat cultivation yields at harvest are approximately seven to eight times their value at time of sowing. In Chile this figure is twelvefold, in North America it is sevenfold, in Peru it is twentyfold, in Southern Mexico twenty-five- to thirty-fivefold. There you have relative wheat yields from land cultivation in various regions of the globe. This fundamentally affects the amount of labour required to convert wheat into commodities to be circulated within the economy.

Just as the amount of labour required to convert wheat into consumables in differing regions can be calculated in terms of the overall economy of a given society, labour levels required in widely differing branches of industry to convert raw materials into finished products can also be determined. This comprehensive entirety is run by means of processes originating in the relationship between human being and nature and are advanced through all that humans contribute to processing natural products into a state of consumer-readiness. Every stage in that all-inclusive sequence from nature to consumer-readiness—and only these—are encompassed within a healthy, purely economic-commercial sphere in a structured society. This sphere of the economy within society as a whole ought to exist self-sufficiently, be self-contained, have some similarity with the way in which the head exists with a degree of independence in the human organism.

In similar independence, alongside the sphere of the economy, another structure ought to be instated, one concerned with inter-human relationships. What is active purely within the economy concerns the need for this or that commodity, which in turn objectifies the human-to-commodity relationship. The second area, however, which ought to develop if a healthy society as a whole is to *awaken,* is all that governs human-to-human relationships.

We have failed to acquire an appropriate view of the differences between these two societal areas. This is because, as if hypnotized or mesmerized, we have been continuing into modern times to believe long-obsolete habits of thought that claim economic forces and processes to be either for individual fields of activity or, in the radical Socialist sense, that all industry can simply be transferred into what I have today described as the second of these spheres—that of the state, in its restricted sense—with its associated domain of public rights legislature and individual-to-individual relations.

This state area will only be capable of evolving wholesomely if it incorporates its converse evolutionary stream. This is seen by some as the only proper course. While many people today believe that restoring the social organism to health is possible only by means of the greatest possible state control—by maximizing communization, taking into common ownership—it is much more a matter of acknowledging, and knowing how to implement, thoroughgoing independence between, on the one hand, the economy with its laws, and on the other the inherent but limited lawfulness of state jurisdiction and its legislature.

I can well imagine how many people may say: For heaven's sake, how complicated does this have to be? What was supposed to be brought together—agglomerated in terms of the requirements of contemporary life—is now to be laid out in separate systems? Those finding this too complex and who are unable to imagine that what accords with nature can become a reality are like someone who doesn't wish to know that human beings can only remain alive because their rhythmic- breathing-and-cardiac system is centred—with a degree of independence—in their rib cage. The entire human organism is reliant on the fact that each such system functions self-sufficiently yet works in harmony with the overall whole. The health of the social organism is reliant on an economy abiding by its own imperatives and the domain of rights—the functioning of public legal rights and security, everything designated in a limited sense as politics—also adhering to its inherent lawfulness and infrastructure. It is precisely then that these two societal domains will work together properly. Those who presume to believe they have reached some ultimate verity may shudder when I say, as indeed I must: Society will not be restored to health as long as the economy and politics are centrally controlled by a single body or party. We will see that this also applies to the third, cultural element. It is essential to appreciate that, just as the circulatory system has its lungs, the nerve-sense system has its cranial networks, that an organ of governance with independent representative bodies, be that parties or other delegated bodies, is in place both for the economy and for politics with its legislature, public rights etc. and—again independently—for the third area, that of spiritual-cultural activity.

Each of these three spheres retains a certain sovereignty within a healthy social coalition and deals with each other through independent representation so that in this structured way their mutual relations are created and maintained within the social fabric. Within its own distinct terms, this corresponds with the human being's naturally threefold constitution. It will transpire that such representation and governance as will emerge from the economic sphere will need to aim for an economy that is developed on *associative* foundations, with co-operatives, collectives, trades unions—albeit elevated versions of these—that is, such associative bodies and unions as only concern themselves with the laws of production, circulation and consumption of goods. Being associatively based will ensure a sound foundation and appropriate content matter for the commercial-economic branch of the social organism. It is upon this associative basis that inequities inevitably arising from discrepancies in natural resources will be offset. I have mentioned how varied human labour quotients can be, dependent as they are on the natural resources required for a given production industry. All this is conflated into an unnatural social structure if nature, human labour and capital are chaotically thrown together in the way that they have been to date. Confusion about natural resources, human labour and capital has been compounded within the single, centralized state or these have remained anarchically outside state influence. It needs to be acknowledged that spiritual-cultural activity is also reliant on the physical and spiritual-intellectual capacities of human beings and their education, and this applies likewise to the public-official political-and-rights sphere, where they have the specific task of separating out and allocating to each a sphere of activity that is independent of all that constitutes the economy.

In order to make myself better understood—to the extent that this is necessary today—I could reach for the following. When the call to reshape society arose out of the deepest substrata of human nature—admittedly from fundaments other than those underpinning our present lives—the slogan of that transformation was expressed in three words: Freedom, Equality, Fraternity.[11] When you approach this without prejudice and with an empathic feeling for humanity and everything truly human, you can do no other than have the deepest sympathy and understanding for everything entailed in those words Freedom, Equality and Fraternity. Yet I know distinguished thinkers—highly astute, deep thinkers—who ever and again throughout the nineteenth century made strenuous efforts to demonstrate how impossible it is to inject into a unified society the ideals of freedom, equality and fraternity and to implement them in everyday reality. A clever Hungarian sought to prove that these three ideals—if they are to become reality, if they are to pervade social structures—are in fact paradoxical. For example, he shrewdly showed how impossible it is to instate equality in the social sphere alone because the feeling for freedom necessarily inherent in each person also has to be acknowledged. He found these three ideals contradictory. Oddly enough, you can't argue with those who note these inconsistencies and you can do no other than extend to each of these ideals your generalized human sympathy! Why is this so?

Well, precisely for the reason that you only understand these three ideals if you also acknowledge as necessary the division of society into three distinct spheres. These three spheres ought not be centralized nor merged into some abstract, theoretical 'Reichstag' or other random assembly, but should be a living reality which, only once working in parallel, then forms a unity grounded in reality. When these three elements are independent, they are in some respects paradoxical, just as the metabolic system gainsays systems of head and rhythmic-breathing. But in life contradictory elements can in tandem create unity. That is why a concept encompassing the life of the social organism will be arrived at once we are in a position to see ahead to an image of society that is congruous with reality. It will then be recognized how in people's co-operative work in industry—where they can legislate among themselves, in their own specific work areas, within this first sector in society—it is fraternity or brotherliness that must be the decisive factor among them. In the second sector, that of public legal rights and so on—where inter-human relationships are prime—it is only to the extent that we are human at all that we would be actualizing the ideal of equality. And in the spiritual area—which also has to be relatively independent within society—the concept of freedom is the watchword. Once you recognize that you cannot make real what has been mixed into a chaotic vortex, these three golden ideals suddenly achieve their full stature as realities. Only in a reality-orientated tripartite social organism can each individual sector achieve the ideal apportioned to them: freedom, equality and fraternity can then be made a reality.

Today I can only sketch out the structure of a social organism. I will enlarge on this and furnish more detailed proof and substance in the next lectures. What I can add to what has already been said, however, is that the third, spiritual sphere of a healthy society must contain all that emanates into it from the human individuality, all of which must be founded upon freedom, something that is in turn based on the physical and spiritual talent or endowment of each individual person. Here we are again touching on an area which, when correctly conceived, admittedly still quietly causes some contemporary folk to quake. What has to be encompassed by this third sphere of a healthy society is everything connected with religious activity, everything concerned with schools, education in its widest sense, all that touches on the creation of the arts and so on. I will only mention this in passing today but will elaborate on it more fully in the next lectures.

The above belongs within a sphere *not* concerned with the public rights law of the second sphere. But the spiritual-intellectual sphere *does* include private law and criminal justice. When presenting this threefold concept of society, I have encountered some who have understood some measure of its structure but who just could not grasp that public-official legislature connected with the security and equality of all people needs to be separated from rights vouchsafed in cases of rights violations or infringements, rights affecting relations between *private individuals*, and that these need to be structured so that *private* and *criminal law* be assigned to the third, intellectual sphere.

Unfortunately, modern life has so far utterly turned its back on considering any societal threefolding. Just as the economy and its interests have forced their way into state—or actually political—ambits and devolved those interests onto representative bodies in political life, thereby damaging any chance of shaping the second societal element consistent with an equality realistically embodied between all individuals; so, likewise, do economy and state extract—siphon off—what can only evolve in a sphere of freedom. Contemporary social democracy has attempted—at the promptings of certain instincts, albeit false instincts—to separate religion from public-official-state life—'religion is a private matter'—but unfortunately not out of deference for religion nor by especially valuing what religion can contribute to human life, but out of a decided contempt for, and indifference towards, all religious activity. All this is connected with what I was saying in the lecture of the day before yesterday.

What is correct in this stance is the separation of religion from the other two spheres of living: from the reach of the economy, from the scope of politics. It is equally vital to separate all primary, secondary, tertiary and higher education—as indeed every possible kind of spiritual-cultural activity—from the other two spheres.

The social organism will be wholesomely structured only if supervisory bodies charged with vouchsafing equal rights for everyone before the law would grasp that solely at the behest of free individuals can schools, religion and all spiritual life thrive; and only when such supervisory bodies as are tasked with ensuring that these activities evolve in freedom, understand—crucially—that this can only happen when neither state nor economy demand that they themselves be allowed to regulate schools, education and spiritual-culture as a whole.

That may seem radical today. But you have to express radicalism of this kind the moment you recognize it. Underlying spiritual life to a vast extent—and this includes all education, the right to free speech in matters of private law and criminal justice—is what flows from people's individuality in complete freedom, so that the other two spheres of society may exert no controlling influence whatsoever over the nature, configuration or content of this spiritual-intellectual cultural sphere.

Today I have only outlined some trains of thought along which attempts at solutions could be directed by way of first steps—such solutions, that is, as are based on life's true essentials, not on the abstract demands of any one party or class, but on humanity-wide forces for progressive evolution.

I'd like to say: I can understand every objection likely to be raised, but I would ask you to suspend these until you have heard, over the coming lectures, how I intend to elaborate on these initial, generalized outlines. I would understand objections, especially today, when I have been trying to describe situations for the viability of which no proof yet exists. But I'd like to add: I can also understand every objection connected with the experience, the knowledge, underlying what I have presented in the form of ideas: ideas which constitute what I believe to be life's *reality base* as derived from the spiritual science so widely underestimated.

Behind us lie times of the most terrible human catastrophe. No humanely-disposed heart could have lived through those catastrophic times without holding out some hopeful prospect, disposition and competence permitting, and wondering: What can help us to extricate ourselves from the frightful chaos towards which we are heading? I said the day before yesterday that I would explore the particular circumstances of the war and its consequences for social problems. In the midst of those events—events that have become an ongoing crisis—is a crisis which some short-term thinkers believe is at an end, that what emerges from the chaos will become calamitous for some regions of the so-called civilized world. To this I will just add that it was clear to me that some proper thinking, some real imagination is required here about what constitutes a truly reality-based impetus towards a wholesome human society. I put the central core of what I have outlined here to some people active in an advisory capacity during those last dreadful years, when so much of a frightful nature took place in human evolution. I tried to put across to these prominent characters, who appeared to be concerned, how different circumstances could be if those leaders with authoritative influence would say to the world: We want to head with all possible speed towards a healthy social order. Then all the relationships between states would have turned out differently. Instead of just legislative-state programmes, a comprehensive agenda benefitting all humanity—in the sense here outlined—could have been introduced in one place or another.

It cannot be claimed that these ideas met with even the slightest theoretical understanding. What I have outlined in these lectures did elicit some sympathy. But the bridge between understanding the ideas and the will to launch them into life in any realistic sense—each in their own area and as appropriate—was a bridge too far. Processes such as these are often uncomfortable. That's why some prefer to block their ears and opine that they come across as an impractical dream scenario. They only block their ears because they lack the requisite will to get a grip on the course of events. I am not proposing a revolutionary course of action nor something that happens overnight in short order, but I am thinking more of a direction with which every single measure in the public and private domain ought to be aligned if the social entity is to be restored.

I put what I have been saying here in a slightly different form to a few individuals with whom it was thought one could reckon, something along the lines of: Here we are, in the most terrible of wars. Were we to frame what appears necessary for human society, we might suggest that you commit to giving content worthy of human beings to this area or another. In doing so, you would to some extent be restoring to health what the terrors of war have wrought—surely a more salutogenic course of action than that of sword or cannon, a better course than the practically non-existent politics of some regions. I said: You have a choice as to whether you acknowledge what is being offered along progressive evolutionary lines. You can make this a reality. Or you can be faced with something quite different.

Because humanity has, in the last decades, largely failed to recognize what is entailed here, we find ourselves in the midst of the most dreadful cataclysm, which has broken over us like a disease, like a pathology overwhelming an entity in conflict with its own naturally-inherent laws. This calamitous war ought to illustrate quite clearly what could have been anticipated in advance and yet, because it was not then as pronounced, it was not noticed. It ought to demonstrate what is required in order to repair humanity's social structures. I said to some: With these indications for social evolution you are being given an awareness of what *is willing* to be made a reality over the next twenty to thirty years in the developed world. I am not talking about some programme, nor simply an ideal, but the result of observing the germinal beginnings already present in human beings of what is *willing* to be made a reality over the coming twenty to thirty years. You only have to choose between using reason to work at making real these ideas or face seeing social revolution, failure and upheaval.

There is no third option. I suggested that war might be the very time to adopt a rational approach. Later on might be too late; because this is not a matter of some package of measures which can be taken up or simply ignored. It is a matter of needing to recognize what is *willing* to be embodied in reality because it is alive as historic potential for forces of growth in the present and the near future.

What proved to be a particular obstacle to their understanding was that a few persisted in believing that these ideas are applicable only to the internal configuration of nations or territories. No, this social thinking is also essentially a basis for international affairs and foreign policy. Just as the human organism and its systems interrelate with the external world through particular organs, likewise must the state—if I may use this generic term—as a social organism transform its three systems into outward-facing action. Relations between individual states transpire quite differently whether centralized government and administrations enter relations or whether representatives of a social sphere—such as the spiritual-intellectual—interact with their opposite numbers among the other nations' intellectual-cultural representatives. Likewise between representatives of economic-industrial and political spheres. While the conflation of the three societal areas remain in confused disarray, the outward effect is such that, if I may phrase it thus, conflicts are bound to erupt on borders where the three spheres remain chaotically admixed. Whereas cross-border contact between individual states, where delegated representatives of the separate spheres are allowed to interact independently in international relations, results in relationships not being damaged but, conversely, being repaired and harmonized.

This is what I wanted to sketch out; something admittedly not intended to reinforce what are, after all, largely matters of a state's domestic social configuration, but which is more concerned with societal life across international humanity. I tried to throw light on this while we were all engulfed in recent desperate events. Whole swathes of people in Central and Eastern Europe are presently experiencing terrible hardship, which to each individual, to each perceptive person, must seem a globally threatening disaster. The following needs to sink in, as regards our universal understanding of our present and future tasks: that those acting out of truly humane evolutionary imperatives in their longing to restore life to health must not be considered impractical idealists but at last be recognized as being the really life-savvy practical people. Technology and capitalism's obvious manipulation of modern life needs to be challenged and confronted by a newly configured and independent spiritual culture, founded upon initiative of the most inward quality, with an independent state culture supportive of the equality between human beings, which will also—as we will shortly see—regulate work- and pay relations in a way advantageous to the proletariat.

The question as to how to reform and liberate human labour from commodification will only be resolved once threefolding is introduced into society. What modern socialists want is certainly justified in terms of willed intention. However, what they themselves see as the remedy would be the very least effective cure if transposed onto reality in the way they envisage.

I would like to emphasize once again: what I say is not said out of any one-sidedly classist or partisan position but is based on observing forces of evolution when talking about what some call a healthy political sense for socializing, others for healing, still others for reawakening society. What underlies the entire thrust and direction of these lectures is that we are not dealing with some arbitrary programme or scheme; we are not dealing with the intentions or opinions of any one rank or echelon; it is a matter of tapping into what prompts the deepest, most realistic impetus for the coming decades in human evolution. This is what I want to present, to elaborate in more detail and to prove over the course of the next two lectures next week. What is expressed here represents the deeper substructure of humanity's will for the coming decades. This I now want to establish and elaborate with more detail and corroboration in next week's two lectures.

Lecture 3

Zurich, 10 February 1919

Zealotry and realism in social thinking and will

In last week's lectures I drew attention to the fact that the present social situation as regards its evolution is experiencing obstacles and difficulties and that much understanding between the various strata or classes among present-day humanity lies quite a long way off. The leading echelons of populations—and the way in which they have evolved over the past centuries and decades into the present—exhibit distinct habits of thought and inner motivation, on the basis of which they tend to sense, think and will. You might say that a chasm exists between these habitual thought patterns and what I described last week as having evolved into the specific idiosyncrasies of the contemporary proletarian way of thinking: how therein lies the source of what is today referred to as the social challenge.

To anyone making the effort to grasp real life robustly, anyone delving into the forces playing out in society's human nexus, it seems far more important to observe these underlying impulses—one might say the motivation below the consciousness with which matters are discussed—than just noting what rises to consciousness. Within those pensive circles of bourgeois citizenry, a whole range of views can be heard. You can also listen to the views current among leading figures of the proletariat. You won't learn very much in the way of realistic world perspectives nor will you deduce much about present social realities by noting those views, other than detecting to some extent what lies behind them. And herein lies far more social psychology and soul lore than both factions imagine.

Some have made efforts to scrutinize from all angles these habits of thought—and I may include myself since I am trying to present them here—on the one hand the habitual thinking among leading bourgeois citizens, on the other those emotive impulses among aspiring proletarians. They will know how wide the gulf is between them, how hard in terms of understanding. This lack of understanding is of historic proportions and is itself a social factor in the present. Here again we see a Bern–Paris axis.[12] If you have a sense for absorbing things of this sort, you may reflect that such completely different languages are heard in each of these places that you might wonder whether what is said in one place can even remotely be understood in the other, and vice versa. That is also why it is presently so difficult to direct your focus—in both bourgeois and proletarian circles—to the main forces driving what is of prime consequence among social issues. Because, in what takes place historically, not everything is of equal importance and because, among historical events, there are those decisive moments which point to the forces actively at work. Other aspects, those sometimes thought by the superficial observer to be equally important, do not really figure in terms of true reality.

Those in a position to follow the proletarian movement properly over past decades will treat as significant the fact that, among much else, workers have taken on board what motivates them—I must admit—in a really scientific manner. And this current proletariat has understood, on the basis of their world outlooks, how to resolve the issues that have brought about their present situation, namely, that issues cropping up in the timeworn stratification of populations into classes or echelons in what used to constitute the old economic and societal order, have to be dissolved over time and replaced with something new.

This is a fact derided by some detractors, who will not be indulged here. Instead, its historical gravity will be highlighted. Maybe what follows was more prevalent in the early days of being aware of the social movement than latterly, when a better accommodation with it was reached. But whenever the issue was discussed with perceptive representatives of a proletarian stance, when the question arose as to the optimum image of society and communal life, according to their lights, and how it might be achieved, the answer was always consistent with that outlook: We have no further interest in this at present. Our primary aim is the dissolution of the existing social order, causing society to implode and so on ad absurdum. What is to replace it will emerge of its own accord. For them it is always a matter of presenting this stance with a view to seizing power and occupying ruling positions. Having successfully vanquished the class marching ahead of them, with power resting in their hands, suitable means would be found and there was no point worrying in advance.

That is programmatic, yet not in any applicable sense. It is also agitator-like. Crucially, it cannot be thought of as consistent with reality. For those with a sense for history's evolutionary potentialities, being consistent with reality entails the question: What does this proletarian attitude signify in evolutionary terms? Here you are forever diverted and deflected because the views themselves are not the prime focus. As I say, it is not what they say about relating to their own feelings, how they experience their lives, what they think about other rankings in society. In short, you are diverted from questions into the status of proletarian life itself. What you largely face in actual life is: not talking, not expressing emotion, but you encounter the life-conditioned existence of a sector of society which, because of how it is, tells you how it is. The answer given by reality, which the living proletariat, as constituted today, itself gives might be formulated as follows. Modern working people, with their opportunities and living conditions, how they are positioned among the structures of modern society, how they feel about being thus situated, experience themselves as being *critics* of the technological and capitalist forms the economy has assumed.

If you have a sense for reality-congruent perspectives, I think it remarkably interesting that an answer can be found among blue-collar workers themselves. Because what exists there—not theoretically, not abstractly debateable—is *criticism*. That the proletariat have become what they are implies a degree of criticism of what exists outside their milieu, criticism of being in the pay of what the economic order has created.

Because this is so, an inherently abstract doctrine—you might almost like to call it a dogma doing the rounds on scientific stilts—but still an orthodoxy, that a creed suffused with basic motivations already present among them has, as just described, taken extremely strong root among workers in the form of Karl Marx's theory. This is a unique instance in the spiritual history of humankind of a scientific theory being taken up by a fresh and unspent segment of humanity, a sector not yet rendered decadent, a stratum having such unexpended reservoirs of intellectuality, such full hearts, such open souls, as though the active ingredient were their very own life forces. This is what has been happening within the proletariat of modern times in its embrace of Marxist teaching.

It is in this respect that a study of real life is vital. You have to have experienced the most gruelling situations—scenarios regarded by other classes as testing to observe. It is into the primarily feeling, perceptive souls of millions upon millions of workers that a seemingly theoretical doctrine has found its way. What does this theoretical doctrine contain? Again, this is the strange thing: it doesn't contain what you would normally call social ideals. It contains nothing by way of a formula, a model for a state of the future, nor indeed how social structuring ought to look. It is, basically, a critique of contemporary bourgeois societal structures and economic configuration. Underlying this Marxist creed to a large extent is *instinct.* Were I to signpost the proletariat towards criticizing technology and capitalist economic models, I would be pointing it towards the reality of its own life. The reality expressed in Marxist ideology is largely a reflection of immediate working existence. Those who believe that Marxist ideology is dismissed by the proletariat don't understand, on the one hand, that external prescriptions, outlooks and concepts can long have been superseded while still retaining their exclusive panache, keeping alive their special impetus while, on the other hand, the opposite view—also Marxist—might have dawned: that the various revisionist attempts might merely represent a continuation of the Marxist ideology already received.

This outlines a social fact which seems to me more important than the rudimentary discussions being widely fostered, because it points to social psychology. And whereas it gives no direct answer, it does relate to our present inquiry from the standpoint of what is probably at the forefront of real-life concerns. We will see over the course of these lectures what can be provided by way of an answer to this.

What impression do you have when you look at facts as they stand open-mindedly and without prejudice? You sense that life as a whole shows a particular foible or idiosyncrasy. Modern living is susceptible to habitual patterns of thought, has developed forms of thinking tending in directions that have proved extraordinarily fertile for natural science. I have often pointed this out in talks, elsewhere and here in Zurich. This thinking trope has been seeking to extend into theorizing and conceptually reforming—or reforming conceptualizations of—social life itself, social phenomena and motivation in life. Throughout this penetrative thinking you have a feeling that present-day people whose thinking is steeped in habitual thought forms do not possess the conceptual capacity to fully grasp the reality of social life's complex phenomena. To some extent the concepts are too tightly intermeshed and cannot themselves capture the complex manifestations of societal life. They remain abstract, they remain mere contours that fail to penetrate the reality of daily life taking place in the body social. One is inclined to say that contemporary humanity is typified by short-termist, stop-gap thinking. This myopic thinking is such that it always disengages the minute you want to delve more deeply into actual life. Thinking of this type has migrated into the aspirations of the proletariat of recent times. That is why such thinking can extend only as far as criticism but not as far as really shaping—on a basis of genuine soul experience—what could serve as a directive force for future orientation. And yet that thinking simply detaches whenever there is a need to aspire to initiative.

In this we are identifying something that cuts deeply into all present life. Those able to seriously determine what present times need will do well to cast their eye in the direction of the view here touched upon, especially at this moment in world history when there is little time for theoretical discussion because the facts are of searing urgency. At this very moment we see how people are faced with urgent, burning actualities, and how this singularity in thinking proves it cannot plumb factual reality. People are often endowed with great goodwill but not with thinking equal to that reality. It is at such historic moments that those able to fathom the signs of the times note the rise of a tendency often masked behind other, quite unconscious traits, a tendency—when faced with burning issues—

that can be especially dire: the rise of a certain hysterically swarming mass zealotry, as I might call it. It is this zealous mindset, which can appear in the most varied guises and fields, which prevents us from intervening appropriately in present circumstances. This blind zeal has arisen out of developments about which I spoke in last week's lectures and which began during the fourteenth, fifteenth and sixteenth centuries.

What constitute the essentials of this unfocused zealotry? These lie in certain unrealistic concepts about life, conceptions from which is missing what I called last week an inner impulse or force of motivation; that in this particular outlook soulful, thoughtful, scientific knowledge-seeking inner activity will somehow seek an island—or continually seek a multitude of islands—but which lacks the will to build a bridge with everyday life. We find that many people today consider it—if I may use the expression—inwardly genteel to adopt a bookish abstraction when mulling over all manner of ethical-religious problems in cloud cuckoo land. We see how people think about the ways in which they can acquire virtues, how they should relate lovingly towards their fellow humans and how they can live a blessed life. We see ideas about redemption, grace and so on developing, ideas which want to maintain all the props to their outlook on life as remotely as possible in soul-spiritual loftiness. At the same time we see an inability to build genuine bridges from everything people hold to be good, loving, well-intentioned, righteous and moral across to what surrounds us in external, everyday reality in the form of capital, working salaries, consumption, production in relation to the circulation of commodities and the banking, credit and fiscal systems. We see how two universal streams are similarly contrasted as regards habitual thinking: one of these streams largely wishes to remain aloft in divine-spiritual heights, is averse to building bridges between religious edicts and the practices of common commerce. Life, however, is a unity, a coherent whole. Life can only flourish if the forces driving it and all ethical-religious aspects are also decanted downwards into the most mundane, quotidian aspects of daily living, into living that simply turns out to be less genteel. If we neglect to make that bridge we regress—as regards religion and ethics—into zealous fanaticism, far removed from true daily reality, and this then takes its revenge. Out of a certain religiosity, people strive for all manner of ideals, for what they consider 'good'. Yet instincts—similarly to basic daily needs which have satisfaction as their fulfilment—originate as they must in economics. Human beings face these instincts toothlessly, unquestioningly and bereft of feeling. They do not know how to bridge the gap between divine grace and mundane proceedings. These latter avenge themselves, taking on a form that wants nothing to do with ethical promptings, with anything wishing to be held in more genteel soul-spiritual loftiness. Revenge, however, will then be such that because ethical-religious considerations have been kept at arm's length from immediate everyday practicalities, revenge will imperceptibly become deceit masked by life: a life-sized inner lie.

How often do we see people going about, the ethical-religious gentility worn on their sleeves displaying—or so they think—their best intentions to live harmoniously with their fellow humans, wishing them only their most benign best, yet failing in this because they lack real social feeling grounded in practical life?

This is how we experience it now, at this—if I may use the term again—world-historic moment, when social issues so visibly, so palpably, crowd in upon us from all sides and where zealous fantasists—who tend to consider themselves the practical ones—are inclined to say: People need to turn their backs on materialism and external, material life, which has caused us no end of trouble and disaster; we need to return to some kind of spirituality, to some spiritual concept of living. You will never tire of quoting or listing the people who talk about the spirituality of the past and, as a rule, it is about the past because it is harder to be even-handed about the present. In fact, you will find that when someone tries to point to what is as essential to practical life as bread, the first thing they will mention is how vital it is that people return to spirituality. This counsel bears a great deal of responsibility for what has led humanity into the present disaster. It is also full of fanaticism masquerading under its many guises and affecting truth. Certainly, a person is delusional if—without knowing external practical conditions—they set up some Utopian social ideal[13] in which they demonstrate the system they have refined and crystallized out to ensure that people live happily, in contented bliss or some such state. Basically, though, these Utopias may be extremely clever, yet it is not about cleverness—nor even of goodwill—but of how they relate to experience in practical life. Nowadays, it is not a matter of telling people to return to spirituality but rather that spirit should inhabit their very thinking about society. It all depends on the *how* of the thinking. As far as I'm concerned, don't mention spirit at all; but let there be spirit in the way you speak about practical life! This will serve present times far better than telling people—zealously, in every other sentence—to return to the spirit. Such people are usually unable to imagine the 'spirit' to whom you might speak, because they cannot rightly imagine spirit at all. The Utopias they set up—and there are more than a few of these—and those finely crafted social ideals are not even their worst symptom, because they are not generally held in much regard. Just how impractical and remote from real-life conditions are the schemes they dream up can readily be seen. Far worse for real life is the veiled ranting seemingly reality-based but actually just nebulous abstraction. We have experienced this zealous fantasizing—let's not be lily-livered about it—only too often in recent events. It goes unrecognized because we have not sufficiently honed our scrutiny of it.

By the way, let us not say anything against the other qualities fantasists may have; they may in many respects be good people, they may carry out their duties in their own areas and be outstanding people. But with regard to personalities of largely fantastical outlook, if you mention that they are behaving fanatically, they tend to be amazed because—so they imagine—they possess obvious powers of discernment. Yet, in reality, the opinions so obvious to themselves amount to little more than *superstition*. For example, over the past few years, I have been watching several practical people—I say this in quotation marks—with a view to identifying fantastical tendencies. In this regard humanity will have to experience a degree of contradiction if it wishes to make progress towards genuine knowledge. It may astound you if I place Ludendorff[14] among the most eminent of fantasists. Both his supporters and detractors opine quite the reverse. The essential quality of his personality—with the exception of the subjects in which he shone academically—was that he was, in all his other thinking, first and foremost a strategic abstractionist. Quite remote from life, he distilled zealous ideas that had nothing to do with reality, doing untold harm in trying to impose these notions onto real life. Personalities such as this, who typify uncompromising fanaticism, wreak a great deal of harm because they are deemed practical people.

In the 1890s there was a veritable epidemic of zealotry. It originated in America and engulfed Europe in the form of what was then called The Society for Ethical Culture[15]. Through ethical pressure, it attempted to spread a culture that was in fact remote from life, despite it being genteel, theoretical sentiment. When anyone mentioned, as I had to, that this amounted to otherworldly fanaticism that trapped and constricted thinking, rendering it unable to drill down into reality, the result was in turns not being understood, being misunderstood or being derided.

This sort of thinking needs to be contrasted with thinking that accords with reality. I believe such thinking has for many years been epitomized by the incisive thinking of spiritual science. What is a crucial feature of a spiritual-scientific world conception? One vital aspect is that it doesn't speak of spirit in terms which merely reflect the external sensory world, but as arising from a genuine experience of a world which is just as real as if it were seen with eyes, heard with ears and touched with hands. It is far less a matter of what is said in theoretical detail about this spiritual world and far more a matter of acquiring an inner cast of soul from spiritual-scientific sources, through which you will know yourselves to be alive as soul-spiritual entities in a real spiritual world. It is not a matter of what you say *about* a spiritual world but of how you experience yourself to be existing within it. You may well believe in some supra-sensory world or other. This can lead to fanaticism despite being born of goodwill. What really matters—while thinking the thoughts that flash through your mind and sensing the feelings which resonate inwardly—is that spirit is actively alive.

This living, active spirit does inhabit us. It is there, just as objects surround us in space and processes surround us in time. If you not only think yourselves into genuine spiritual knowledge but also *live* into it, then an inner impetus will spring from this spiritual source, an incentive to make the spirit real in the world through yourselves; the will to experience the spirit as a reality and to actualize it completely differently from the way it can exist as just a mirror image of ideas and concepts *about* the spirit. There is a great difference between *thinking about* the spirit, *believing in* the spirit and *experiencing* that spirit thinks in me, spirit senses in me. The traditional concept of belief actually becomes meaningless in the face of this experience. Some soul-spiritual strength has to flow into human evolution from this experience. And this element of soul-spiritual strength, which needs to flow into human evolution, is of greater social significance than you can possibly imagine. This is because it has far greater power to heal the paralysing ideology described here last week, ideology which the proletariat has inherited from the bourgeoisie as an oppressive legacy.

This is really behind the first true form of the social challenge, if one is able to plumb its depths: that the evolution of spiritual life since the turn of recent times in the fourteenth century has become ever more curtailed, attenuated and debilitated, so that people no longer know that 'living spirit truly inhabits me', but they have instead begun to believe that only ideas reflecting reality can inhabit them. This has become the view and life perspective of the proletariat to the extent that they claim that only ideology can exist at a spiritual level. Reality consists only of economic processes and class warfare—that is where reality takes place. From this view of the world something, as it were, seethes upwards into human souls in the form of revelatory imagery, impressions originating in science, in ethics, in religion and the arts, providing super-constructs for what has to be the only genuine substructure. Even if you cannot avoid admitting that what exists in this sociological super-construct is just an ideology, it does nevertheless remain an ideology. And ideology can provide no remedy. There is no restoration if you are unable to attain to genuine spiritual experience in the form in which spiritual science wishes to introduce it into humanity. Healing the harm caused by ideology can only be effected by deep immersion in the true supra-sensory world of spirit and all that it manifests.

Culture leads people into spirituality. Yet due to what has caused anything spiritual to be considered mere ideology, proletarians are left without that certain feeling of confident elan or panache that results from an individual being conscious of what they really are in the sense of their higher identity. And because ideology is insubstantial and spectral, they remain dissatisfied and lacking a full sense of worth. It is out of this bleak state that the desolate mood has grown which typifies the proletarian world outlook, forming one aspect of present social issues. As long as there is no insight into the fact that the human tendency towards ideology needs to be rehabilitated, it will not be possible to bring positive stimulus to working people. All that will then remain is criticism of techno-capitalist economics and attendant world views.

This is why a genuinely practical outlook will not be established if there is no will to introduce a world view not just containing theories and religious notions, but which is alive, which longs to generate life and to give birth to life-enhancing initiative. For this to happen, something is required at whose apparent radicalism some modern people may baulk. However, what is proposed here is far less radical than what life itself will unleash into contemporary instincts if people are too complacent to turn to what is required.

What I have been sketching out from a specific perspective since last Wednesday relates to one sphere of the social organism and needs to take shape out of present conditions and right across the spectrum of human experience. I argued that if humankind's misfortunes are not acknowledged—and they are not—then here is the crux: spheres of influence which ought to be tripartite or threefold in structure—that is, relatively independent of each other while still interacting dynamically—are presently thrown together in a single chaotic agglomeration, which is bound to set the future awry.

So as not to be misunderstood, let me reiterate that I am in all truth *not* advocating some rebellious upheaval overnight. What I am offering are guidelines—directions of flow—by which questions of spiritual culture, state and economic-industrial activity can find some orientation which is available to everyone. There is no need instantly to believe—as do some with whom I have discussed this—that what is today thought of as the state must be turned into something different tomorrow. You just need to have the *will* for these things, to apply in reality the Christian challenge to 'transform yourself'—in other words to thoroughly align yourselves with such measures as are presented to you and to take action whenever you are called upon to steer matters in a definite direction.

This is what I am putting forward. What is jumbled together today within the unitary state—thrown together like a human reconfigured as a Homunculus[16] so that its three systems are randomly centralized in an overarching state business—ought now to be dynamically disassembled and restored to balance in the form of a threefold societal organism. Both what has evolved as spiritual-intellectual culture, as well as everything known in its limited sense as the political state, need to become independent, decentralized elements, interacting in dynamic mutuality. And as a third element, an economic sphere must also evolve independently. Spiritual sphere, state sphere, economic sphere: it is towards these three that human effort needs to be working over the next twenty to thirty years. Those who oppose this evolution are opposing the very life-potential of present humanity.

In laying out from this perspective what has been touched upon today, I initially identified a sphere we can call spiritual-intellectual culture, which includes everything to do with schools, educational bodies, religious activity, everything comprising artistic and literary endeavour, as also what pertains to private-civil and criminal law. I will describe these latter more fully later. Everything included within this area of spiritual culture must be founded on a communal yet independent basis, one differing from the bases upon which the other two societal spheres are posited. It needs to exist self-sufficiently, grounded in such a way that the following is true. The vital quality in this sphere of society must chime with forces freely unfolding the physical and spiritual potential at the core of each and every individual. Everything in this sphere has to be centred around individuality, because all creativity in this realm flows from the individual. Their physical and spiritual potential must have free rein to develop whilst also being prevented from harming, inhibiting or unduly interfering in the rest of culture.

Much could be said in this respect. I would just like to bring one peculiar example to your attention. I'm sorry if this example seems slightly preposterous but it may express what I wish to say about this cultural sphere. Let's say that an aspiring young student in the midst of academic life is studying for a doctorate. S/he is advised by a supervisor to work on an as yet little researched subject, let's say on words of abuse in the works of some Roman writer. This does happen, as you may know. So this young student spends a year working on the terms of abuse in the works of a Roman writer. Today this might well be thought academically important. Indeed, in terms of perspectives rife in academic fields, it might well be thought scientifically significant. But something else has to be taken into account: how does this affect the social organism as a whole? You have to ignore this question if you want to find some old Roman's swearwords fascinating. I know of no dissertation on the use of parentheses by an ancient Greek writer over which a young student has slaved. I do not wish to speak ill of work that may contain intellectual objectivity, neither do I wish to endorse any banal utilitarianism. In terms of relevance for society, students may spend a year or so in the most diligent studiousness, but they will also need to eat, drink, be clothed and have some income or capital funding. What does this mean? Will they devour a pile of capital? In real life this can only mean that very many other people will have to work on their behalf. What they eat, what they drink, how their clothes are provided, will employ a whole host of people over the course of a year. They engage a small army of people to supply their food, drink and clothes, and this becomes considerable in terms of its social effects. Nowadays, you may be persuaded that you are simply serving academic interests by putting such papers out into the world without any social understanding. Our present life, however, demands that any branch of society, in its relationship—in its living associations—with all other branches of life has to be alive to social sensitivities.

As I said, I asked for your indulgence in bringing a slightly peculiar example—there could have been less extreme ones—but I used this one to demonstrate to you how essential it is to develop a feeling for the way in which spiritual culture—in its entirety—has to exist within the social organism such that it is justified in terms of humanity's overall interests. It has to be asked whether these general human interests would have placed such value in identifying terms of abuse, as used by that old Roman, as to justify the cost of employing a small army for a year. The question could be framed less extremely if slightly rephrased. Then it might occur to you that what is encompassed by spiritual-academic culture—to which all technical innovation also belongs—might have a dynamic effect on other spheres, such as on state- or constitutional legislation, were it to be given greater independence in real life. Centralization, by contrast, has the effect of causing chaos.

Everything in the spiritual-cultural sphere needs to exist largely independently, needs not only to revolve around the inner freedom of individuals, functioning freely and competitively, not beholden to any state monopoly, so that what it accrues by way of popular validation—what this is in terms of individual human endorsement is another matter, here we are talking about how the social organism is shaped—manifests solely in free competition and in freely meeting the needs of the general public. If someone writes poetry in their free time, or seeks friends with whom to share poetry to their heart's content, spiritual life is self-justifying purely in terms of what people wish to co-experience with each other as individuals. This will only be on a wholesome footing if all spiritual endeavour—schools, colleges and universities, all life revolving around education and the experience of art—is divested of anything suggestive of state control and becomes self-sufficient. And, as I said, a direction is being indicated here that is not instantly actionable between now and tomorrow, but will be once individuals are self-reliant enough. In this way, a bridge is also extended to something else. Back in the 1890s I made efforts, in my now reprinted book *The Philosophy of Freedom*,[17] to show in timely manner how the experience of true human freedom can exist solely through genuine spirituality impinging on the human psyche. At the time, I called the intuition flowing into souls an influx of true spirit. This true spirit has to be born in the light of freedom and free competition, and then it will find its way fittingly into the social organism. Crucially, it must remain free of all supervision and control. Nor may it be taken under the aegis of another branch of society because it will only find its true expression in total freedom and in response to universal need.

I will outline this further in coming lectures, but I know that many people believe that, were school to be free, we would all be surrounded by illiterates. I will shortly show that this is not the case. Due to its intrinsic nature, my prime concern today is to show how essential a free cultural-academic sphere is for the social organism. In most countries across the world today science is a monopoly and its business concerns are also monopolized by the state. Here the axiom that 'the tenets of science are free' predominates. This is an empty phrase and will remain so for as long as spiritual-intellectual life is not independent. Not only must spiritual culture be free in respect of the people working within it. But what is permissible to say—or not to say—in public then becomes contingent on another branch of the body social. Yet, as I say, if one of the other spheres takes control of schools and universities—be it appointing or setting limits on staff, dictating what may and may not be said—then even the very content of intellectual endeavour will be subject to control. Our entire scientific establishment has borne the stamp of politics ever since political jurisdiction has been overextending itself, encroaching on intellectual activity. However, spiritual culture cannot be subject to the dictates of any other societal sphere, and can only encompass content appropriate to itself as it evolves out of free human individuality.

Now, one point can be raised ever and again, and I have already mentioned it in these lectures. What is particularly striking in the economy—or rather in proletarians' science-based view of the economy—is that in this regard the proletariat have taken on the legacy of other classes. For reasons previously given, ever since technology and capitalism emerged, people's focus has been as if transfixed by the notion that the economy is society's only valid reality. In evolutionary terms, many believe that economic criteria are the only relevant yardsticks. Yet you have to bear in mind that, contrasting this economic perspective, there is—as we have seen—a commitment to bringing an especially effective impetus into the bright light of day: a feeling for humanity, a feeling for human dignity. It is because of this that Karl Marx had such an incendiary effect on millions upon millions of workers who at first believed that he had clearly been referring to a stance worthy of human dignity inherent among modern proletarians. He, Karl Marx, initially pointed to the fact that, for proletarians, their labour was a commodity[18] like other goods in circulation in the economy and that it was subject to laws of supply and demand.

Karl Marx was pointing—largely erroneously—to the facts underlying this view. That he tapped into this root-nerve of the social issue at all is felt by the proletarian soul to be particularly deserving of merit. Here, too, socio-psychological aspects correspond with reality to a far more significant degree than the theories, interpretations and discussions often associated with working- or social settings. But the existential question then arises: How can what is felt to be worthy of human beings be negotiated if human labour is a commodity and continues to be regarded as goods? This is what Karl Marx asked to begin with. As I said, his approach is deceptive and mistaken in many respects, but that is not the point here, because when even a specious fact has such an enormously motivational thrust affecting the souls of millions of people, it simply becomes a social fact. That is what Karl Marx said and that is how blue-collar workers understood him. This understanding, though it has changed in some regards, still resonates today, working its exceptionally vigorous way into present feelings. According to him: within commercial trade, goods are brought onto the market and sold. There are owners of goods, possessors of goods, buyers of goods. The proletariat possesses nothing other than their own power of labour. Certain essential production costs attach to each commodity. The manufacturing costs of this item or that, through to consumer-readiness, are of such and such a level. Workers possess only their physical strength, their labour. To create this power of labour, everything to do with food, clothing and so on has to be earned. Due to what they have to earn to cover food, clothing, shelter and so forth, the labour involved in this has to be continually replaced. These are the manufacturing costs of their labour. Well, said Karl Marx, and in their inmost core this is what proletarians also believe: uncompelled and uncoerced, an employer does no more than reimburse them for their labour, in the form of what some call recompense for work and manufacturing costs. But supposing, for example, that all those manufacturing costs were worked off—paid off in say five hours—contemporary employers persist in being dissatisfied. They will demand longer working hours. Workers will then be working gratis, for no reward, because they receive only as much as is incurred by the manufacturing costs of their 'commodity' labour. Anything worked over and above these costs is a bonus, is added value. This is what is brought to the altar—if you can call it that—of capitalism, this is what accumulates as capital, but which originates in workers' power of labour and is therefore a result of them only receiving manufacturing costs, because they are forced to tout something they alone can offer under commercial conditions on the labour market: their 'product' in the form of their labour.

You can apply the greatest acuity and have the deepest understanding of political economics in discussing how to bring about a situation where workers no longer need to bring their labour onto the market in the form of a commodity and how to banish this last remnant of slavery from the world. Despite applying to the problem the cleverest wit, political-economic expertise, business acumen and the most profound feelings, it will take you several lifetimes to ponder all this and you will come to no conclusion. You cannot reach any conclusion because this remains—in its most eminent form—a non-discussable issue, one which cannot be theoretically answered, but which only life itself can answer, and then only if something can be created which affects life in such a way that human labour is stripped of its commodified status.

If I may use a comparison, I'd like to refer to the little man in Goethe's *Faust* created by Wagner in his laboratory retort: the Homunculus. He consists of every imaginable component from nature, yet is still only a quasi-humanoid and not a human being. You can assemble constituent understandings or the component-ingredients of political economies, but you will still only create a social Homunculus! Just as you have to create conditions in which a living human can exist, likewise do you have to create conditions in which a thriving social organism can exist, so that in real life human labour is permanently disconnected from theories and arguments and remains distinct from all that goes on in the circulation of goods.

You will achieve this in no other way than by insisting that a dynamic social organism consists of independent entities and, alongside a spiritual sphere, a legislative state—in its limited sense a political-state sphere—and, largely independently alongside these, an economic sector which is bound to abide by its own inherent laws. Just as unable as a stomach is to perform breathing and cause heartbeats, the economic sphere is unable to develop legislation out of its own inherent forces. It will never create legal rights if it only functions according to its own natural foundations. On material foundations such as these the social organism will only function along lines of manufacturing and trade to consumption.

However, in the same way as the circulation of commodities proceeds distinct from nature itself—which is the natural foundation of all production, consumption and all activity relating to crafts, trades and business—similarly must political-legislative organizations exist distinct from—and not determined by—the economy. The economy is to be determined by activity in the political-legal sphere of rights. The latter has to be as independent from the economy as the heart-and-lung system is largely independent of the cranial-nerve-sense system. It is precisely because these areas work independently of one another, while yet co-operating, that they form the right relationship in real life. Only because lung and heart are separated from metabolic-digestive activity in the human body are these relatively distinct functions able to work correctly in partnership. Only by ensuring that in a dynamic social organism there is provision for independent yet interactive entities—not dominated by economic substrata which cause labour to be commodified—can there be assurance that in real-life terms labour is situated among social structures in such a way that it is conceived of as a legal right. Only in this way can you allow the economy to be governed. By the same token, legal rights are vouchsafed by the legislature of a restricted political state and the economy is determined by its foundations in natural resources.

Only once these three spheres can be inaugurated relatively independently alongside each other—an independent spiritual culture, an autonomous legislative-state system of rights, and a self-sufficient economic system—will these three sectors work in self-sustaining reciprocity alongside one another; when each element works in accordance with its own foundational principles, with its own representative governing body—let's say its own government, legislative chambers, assembly or ministry—and these distinct elements relate in mutual relationships that are almost as sovereign as those existing between individual states or nations, dealing solely through delegated powers, only then will the societal organism be truly restored to health. Then, in the economy, bases for interest can develop among principles only possessing decisive powers within that economy.

Then life itself will be able to prompt the following question via processes taking place in another area, in the legal-judicial sphere: If at the incentive of this legal sphere limitations are set on human labour—which from then on will not be defined as a commodity but as a right—and this labour feeds into a particular branch of the economy, causing that branch to become unviable, then the branch concerned will have to be assessed in viability terms in much the same way as over-expensive raw materials may be deemed unviable. This means that labour will become a leading factor in the economy instead of a component that is subjugated or enslaved. However, this will not be achieved just by passing laws but rather by forming an active body in real life which—simply because it is distinct will necessarily contain different imperatives—will forever, epoch after epoch, remove from labour its commodity connotation. Labour must be prised away from being regarded as goods so as to prevent it from continually being sucked into an economy always tending to engulf human labour and reduce it to a product. State bodies must always remain alert to stripping human labour of its commodity status.

On all sides life shows us how the enormous jumble—if you'll excuse the frivolous word—of the three areas in society causes harm. Just look at the terrible consequences for the societal sphere and all the other man-made catastrophes caused over the past four and a half years. Just examine the events themselves. For one graphic example, you could look at Austria and the way in which things have been *atomized*. How have its internal structures been maintained for over half a century? There was a so-called Imperial Council containing certain people's representatives—albeit who represented only selected echelons—which collapsed, not recently but when events were brewing, back in the latter half of the nineteenth century. This disintegrated into four curia or tribunals: those of large-scale land-owners, rural communities, towns-and-markets and industrial cities with their chambers of commerce. In other words: rural communities, towns, landowners and chambers of commerce. You see how sundry basically commercial interests were vested in these delegated bodies, which in turn represented the state. They created legislature. This came about because—as I was mentioning at the start of today's talk—they were completely unconscious of infiltrating the economy with their own organizations because their thinking was so blinkered and myopic in focus as to be incapable of drilling down into reality. They took the ascendant state to be the framework for the economy and hashed together state and economy. Unless people realize that it is in such pooled and tangled messes that the causes of countless disasters lie, including our catastrophic present, genuine remedies will not be found.

Today, again, I was only able to give you a few indications and may be permitted to bring you further elaboration the day after tomorrow. I would just like to say: Even in the context of global politics will you find confirmation of what I have been saying if you are prepared to delve down into life's substrata. Anyone studying the genesis of this terrible war—which is no war in the old sense of the word but a pan-human cataclysm, a brew consisting of innumerable ingredients, a war not nearing its end but entering its critical phase—anyone studying the origins of this disaster will find, for example, that a significant factor at its inception as well as in the preparations leading up to it, was the emergence of the present economic order through unconscious processes ignorant of how to separate out an economy intermixed with a legislative sphere into a viable entity in harmony with its inherent nature, capable of supporting life and applicable across the globe once suitably separate. But state-legislature and the economy remained intermeshed. Basically, then, economic factors and forces exist which have been availing themselves of state powers over the past decades, economic forces working against other influences discordantly. Had they been held to progressing only on a basis of their mutually co-operative activity within the commercial economy, they could never have contributed to this disaster. These purely economic forces were able to lead to this catastrophe because they were allowed to do so by a false embodiment of political-state powers sending their hordes into battle on their behalf.

Matters such as this have to be laid out contextually for consideration, not just theorized about. A few people do this today. But you have to see, in its true light, all that is thronging and burning throughout modern times in relation to the actual impetus of social questions as a symptom. Then you will emerge from zealous fantasizing or swarm-raving and enter the reality which will enable the three elements of the social organism to work together in real life. What no discussion nor appraisal by the political economy can achieve—the parallel coexistence of economy and political-legislature—will resolve the issue of human labour and will be able, rightfully and enduringly, to banish from the world one of the most fundamental and noxious issues in the sensitivities of modern proletarians.

Now, I will continue these reflections the day after tomorrow and go in more detail into such aspects as I have today had to leave open to query, so that they can be suitably clarified.

There is just one more thing I may be allowed to mention. Today's indolent habits of thought—which will persist for some time to come—may entail people considering as too radical, too academic, too remote, what is in fact no abstract idealism but is genuinely practicable experience for life. Some will say: So, here comes one of those spiritual-sciencers, wanting to add their pennyworth to one of the most eminently pertinent, world-historically important conversations, the societal challenge. It is precisely *not* for my own sake nor for the sakes of those standing for the direction I am here representing, but for those people who deem this sort of thing an impractical lost cause, lacking as they do a broad overview or indeed a focused perspective—it is for those people, not for myself, that I want to make a comparison by way of rounding off. I want to draw your attention to that poor boy, Stephenson,[19] who was once compelled to sit on a Newcomen steam engine, opening and shutting inlet valves in alternation, allowing ingress on one side to steam, on the other to condensed water. The boy noticed that the crank of the crankshaft was moving up and down and the thought occurred to him to wonder how it would be if he connected these alternating valves to the crankshaft. Then each valve would open in alternation due to its valve handle being pulled now open, now shut. The crank would replace my work and I could then just watch on, thought the small boy. And this is what he actually did. Something resulted, as often happens when something new is expressed or stated, about which a conventionally clever person might respond: Stupid boy! Just do as you're told. What are these daft attachments on the crankshaft? Take them off right away or you'll be for it. Well, that's not what happened. One of the most significant inventions of the time—self-regulating steam engines—stems from the experience of a small boy. Spiritual science asks no more than to lay claim to having developed an accurate view about the self-regulation—the dynamic and co-operative reciprocal interaction—between the three spheres contained within the social organism, that is: a self-activating cultural-spiritual sphere, a political-judicial sphere and an economy. Now it is a matter of seeing whether those conventionally clever people tell spiritual science: You stupid boy, just stick to your job! Or whether they will themselves commit to it. You often have to remind yourself of this example—in all modesty and without pretension—when in the midst of events. May faith in the practical abilities of zealous fantasists soon makes way for the conviction that the truly practical people in life are those derided idealists who are able to commit to the realities of life, that it is they who have to research the genuine evolutionary conditions of humankind. For it is only by acknowledging the factual implications of these evolutionary conditions and powers that a way can be found to resolve social issues—about which more will be said next time—to the extent possible in real life. It will not be the arrogant ways of those deeming themselves the practical ones who will set the right course, but this will probably fall to those derided idealist-practitioners capable of committing to real life.

Lecture 4

Zurich, 12 February 1919

Evolving social thinking and will in contemporary conditions—two streams

Maybe the lectures I have been permitted to hold here last week and the week before show how, from that perspective, the following statement is justified. Humanity's present situation is profoundly influenced by the evolving course taken by social thinking and willing over recent times and into the present. Nowadays, social catalysts intervene more powerfully into the immediate lives of individuals than you perhaps imagine, but they will interfere ever increasingly in future. They will even challenge the very sovereignty of our most individual conduct. You will find it hard to comprehend how we exist in the midst of societal life—throughout which social impulsions surge and throb—if you don't bear in mind how the social thinking and will of differing social echelons has arisen from two sources over recent times; because the onward flow into the present from those origins gives to modern life its social configuration.

In one of the lectures I mentioned that you won't make progress in understanding a subject such as history if you bring to it only habitual, linear thinking which just runs along lines of effect following cause, so that you are always alluding to the previous from the subsequent. I tried to draw your attention to the fact that, historically, pan-human life is in many essentials analogous with individual lives in that certain sequential crises or, more accurately, the presence of crises in the process of developing, may occur. Individual progress may not unfold in straight lines, such that what follows is, without rifts or leaps, an effect of preceding events. In order to dispatch the comfortable, often mistaken thought that nature makes no leaps outside its limiting parameters, you have to be constantly alert to the fact that in the linear process of individual lives there occur crises such as those around age six or seven, when the change of teeth takes place or the watershed moment when sexual maturity is reached, welling up from elemental, organic depths. Those conversant with the course of human life know that such key crisis-like moments of disruption do take place, also in later years, though not perhaps as dramatically to superficial observation as the two instances cited.

Observing similar upheavals in human history is essential for an understanding of that history. However much present humanity is disinclined to look at, or listen to, any such view, it is fundamental, and understanding social life demands that robust, radical attention be paid to these instances. As I explained previously, one of the last great changes of this kind in human evolution is that which we have to place around the turn of the fifteenth and sixteenth centuries. Because the course of history has not been sufficiently thoroughly researched, it is not acknowledged how radically different what proceeds in the human psyche can be in terms of demands, which longings for specific fulfilment may be exerting influence and how these may have changed since all that preceded them.

Now, at the same time, something emerges in more recent human evolution as if in consequence of this elemental upheaval, something you might characterize as follows. What used to exist at a soul level as a social impetus, and which led to the social structuring of human society, worked more instinctively before the timeframe in question. People lived together socially, managing their affairs socially as prompted at an instinctive level. Around the time mentioned, instinctive social thinking and willing began to be replaced by a more conscious grasp of social stimuli. This emerged gradually over time; yet the life circumstances in which people find themselves as a result differ radically from conditions experienced in the Middle Ages and more remotely ancient times. Here we see how, as social impulses emerge from instinctive levels into consciousness, two clearly distinct streams, two nascent sources, become visible: those of social thinking and social willing.

One of these surfaces among people who can, into present times, be termed leading or pre-eminent echelons or classes in society. The other stream arises somewhat later, but can be clearly differentiated from the first, appearing as it does among what we call the proletariat or working classes. As time goes by, the leading, intellectual, bourgeois circles gradually become connected—together with their interests—with all that takes shape as the more recent forms of state which have evolved from out of medieval forms of societal coexistence. These leading, bourgeois circles are connected through their interests with what I would call—in terms of the three elements of the social organism I introduced earlier—the sphere of law, of legislation, the political fabric itself, the sphere from which everything issues, whether instinctively or consciously, to do with law and order and with inter-human relationships. In much the same way as the traditions of the past came about—likewise, in some respects, more recent economic relations—prominent bourgeois circles link their interests with those of what is thought by many to be today's only social structure: the state. In so far as their awareness moves from the old instinctive social situation to one that is consciously modern, their immediate thinking is state-like; they think in terms of state jurisdiction, constitutional law. Those in pre-eminent circles try to form increasingly complex commercial networks—now extending across the world as human activity widens horizons—into state-like structures. In some respects, they aim increasingly to turn the state into an economist, an economy. This urge takes its course and we see within some groupings how individual branches of industry become ever more subsumed into state structures. I mentioned some of these industrial branches last time. Central to the social thinking current in these circles is the distinctive stamp it bears on account of its wish to conquer for the state—repository of their interests—the increasingly complex economy irrupting into society.

Social motivation develops quite differently among the proletariat. The interests of contemporary proletarians are not vested in the state itself in the same way. Due to time constraints, I cannot elaborate further on this now, but the matter is transparent and is distinct from what the pre-eminent bourgeoisie identify as their interests within state structures. Yet this proletariat is driven in the most radical way into determining the configuration of economic-industrial life. Their entire thinking and willing works as if reflecting what the economy itself is undergoing. Thus, the social impulses of the proletariat are just as conditioned by the social fabric of commercial industry as are the incentives of pre-eminent bourgeois and intellectual circles by the state-legislative sphere, by the body politic itself. As I said when introducing the day before yesterday's lecture, both these streams develop in such a way that a chasm, a veritable abyss, appears between the specific configurations of social thinking and willing, among leading bourgeois circles and their proletarian counterparts. As I said, this chasm is the most tragic aspect of recent developments in humanity's circumstances, an abyss over which it is extremely difficult to broker mutual understanding between the configurations of the two societal strata depicted. That is why what we could see coming had to ensue, namely, both societal strata facing each other as if armed for mortal combat. An essential feature of this battle—which is already to some extent in process, partly only in preparation—and a situation which makes sense, even today only superficially interests society yet will in future assume gigantic proportions. The essential factor, on the one hand, is that leading bourgeois elements increasingly wish to seize economic life for the state and, typically, also wish to control—on behalf of the state—not only the economy but proletarian output and labour as well; while, on the other hand, proletarians want to defeat the state in pursuit of their interests in what they experience as an isolated, segregated economy.

That is essentially the rationale of the confrontation, which plays so mordantly into the circumstances of present humanity. Behind everything proceeding consciously in the open is what has been forgotten, neglected and, I would say, forced down into unconscious recesses of the soul and actually concealed behind the two motivating forces outlined. The impetus which has been waiting to work its way to the surface of human life since the crisis-like reversion of the fifteenth century, when it entered recent evolution, now really surfaces. At the same time, opposing impulsions scrabble, roil and throb, largely masked from human consciousness, struggling for a fully validating endorsement of their own personalities in a way unknown to earlier times. Affirming the human personality, having a feeling for human existence itself, is what actually lies at the root of this social issue, assuming the garb of either of these divergently-conditioned life circumstances, in the differing forms just described. This is how battle—which is fundamentally a battle for the full human dignity of *all* humankind—could arise, could become warfare between two sets of conflicting interests, a battle between classes, a battle which casts the force of its baleful shadow into humanity's social present.

The fact that something masked is manifesting in recent evolution has caused us to fail to focus our attention on—or rather, has been the cause of us not yet learning to discern—what really matters. As long as social impulsion was working at an instinctive level, the social organism as a whole could likewise be left to assume its own form. Now that social motivation has entered people's consciousness, albeit in masked form, it is vital—it is actually *the most vital aspect* of contemporary social tribulations—that social literacy, that understanding the ways in which the social organism is configured, dawns in every single human psyche. This grasp need not be of an academic nature but more on a feeling level, an emotional literacy experienceable in everything an individual holds to be essential. This has to flow into society. That is why it is so important to do what I have been trying to do throughout these lectures: to turn our focus towards what humanity has lately been tending to strive for, but which can only struggle to the surface due to today's unique circumstances: to focus on the need for the social organism to become a dynamic, animated structure, a structure understood not just in theory but in the context of real-life conditions. That is why I said that the health of the social organism depends on its three constituent elements not being chaotically thrown together but organized in the form of an infinitely broad spiritual-cultural element, a judicial-constitutional element—state activity in its restricted sense—and an economic-industrial sector. Only in this way will the forces active in these three areas affect society as they ought, and in doing so undergo their own liberation such that no single element is absorbed by another but can evolve freely in parallel, in relative independence and in mutual co-operation, as already outlined from several angles. Evolving conditions have militated against such tendencies towards independence. Now, disentangling what has been agglomerated is the most pressing task in present social reality.

What I am here describing has always been experienced—from perspectives of thinking or feeling, according to psychic predisposition—when people began, in light of their societal awareness, to establish ideas about the relationship between state and economy. We see the rise of socio- or political-economic tropes and habits of thinking—terms are irrelevant. Describing the evolution of sociological thinking cannot be my task here. I will just draw attention to one thing which, I have to say, throws a stark light on what must be a central leitmotif of these lectures.

Among the myriad ways of thinking about and conceptualizing how economy, state and spiritual culture are intertwined, recent times have seen the appearance of what the eighteenth century termed *Physiocratic* political-economic thinking. This Physiocratic thinking follows from earlier thinking, forming a necessary contrast to the aim of organizing the economy more closely within the state. Its rationale demanded a transition to a position preventing the economy from being tyrannized by the legislative sphere of the state and by the political arm of state structures—in their restricted sense—thereby leaving economic life to its innate natural laws, leaving it to the vagaries to which the economy is subject when people simply act in unrestricted pursuit of their own interests. Advocates of this system actually had some enlightening words to say, which can be paraphrased somewhat as follows. They asked: What is the point in framing a legislative system to regulate the economy within state-political structures? Either these laws will be identical with those governing the economy itself when given free rein within market forces or they will be such that they oppose them. In the first case, if they are identical, framing them will be superfluous; the economy will self-regulate, obviating any need for specialized state legislation. However, if state legislation acts contrary to the economy, then it is a harmful hindrance to it and will detract from it.

I would like to say that what these opposing positions express still haunts many minds. It plagues them because contemporary humanity, however much it believes itself to be practical and have a healthy feeling for reality, is still disastrously sold on a certain abstraction and theoretical one-sidedness. Were you to test what people actually deem practical, you would find nothing other than unilateralism embodied, one-sided theory objectified. You would then have stumbled upon one of life's riddles and be in some part able to explain it. What sounds more plausible, more obvious, than when I claim that either state legislation aligns itself with that of the economy—in which case it is superfluous—or it countermands the economy, in which case it is bound to damage it? You only think in terms of these antitheses if you view the social organism as something which allows itself to be governed by concepts, laws, principles and programmes, when you cannot rise to a level where society can be understood as an entity necessarily containing life and hence obliged to live in accordance with its essential nature. Yet whatever thrives and burgeons on its own impulses will contain paradoxes and disparities in real life. Thus the social organism—if it is be truly realistic—must also embrace contradiction.

So, what many theoretically inclined souls today consider to be absurd is in fact correct: that the purely political legislature of the state must to a certain extent restrict and counteract the economy legally, so that general existence—which is not purely economic nor solely legally framed but rather encompasses commercial, legal and spiritual elements—can flourish in a way similar to elements in individual human bodies. I use this comparison once again in passing and not as if making an exact analogy between physiology and sociology, yet the digestive system is to some degree self-contained alongside a rhythmical breathing-and-cardiac system, both also—in terms of their functional processes—mutually limiting and boundary-defining. In real-life society it is just as crucial to place proximately the economy, on the one hand, and a restricted political state on the other and, consorting with both these largely independently, spiritual culture, as I outlined last time from a slightly different perspective.

Key issues depend on this: economic life contains quite different internal forces from those of the legislative-rights sphere—with which it has to co-operate to the end that comprehensive societal life can flourish—and these forces again differ from those of intellectual-spiritual culture. Were you to frame this in a slightly more tangibly graphic—albeit one-sidedly abstract—way, you could explain it like this: in the economy, as it exists in terms of production, circulation and consumption of goods or commodities, much depends on corresponding values being created in real life. If the social organism is to become wholesome, the creation of this added value is basically such that value has to be created under influence of the motivation that its use, which the economy claims for itself—call it the market or what you will—offers the consumer use of a product that is as fit for purpose and as advantageous as possible. In a healthy social organism, a product that is as useable, practicable and long-lasting as possible has to be offered to the consumer; or indeed goods that can be used suitably quickly, at any rate products that are entirely streamlined towards their functional utility.

Were human labour to be fully engaged in industry—in an economy only capable of evolving vigorously from bases of product-based pricing and consistent with resultant usage—the Marxist claim espoused by the proletariat that human labour would itself become a commodity would be fulfilled. Thus would this labour force, tainted with the label of a commodity, have to maintain its value in the social organism by being fully put to use in the most appropriate way. On closer inspection, the economic sphere of the social organism has a tendency to misuse, in fact to abuse, human beings and, were the economy to be bound solely by its own determinants, human labour would be *exploited.* Because pre-eminent bourgeois circles paid this no heed, they actually contributed to the situation where, between economy and the attitudes of workers, the core issue of present social problems could take shape. This showed its colours particularly in proletarians taking considerable exception to their labour being regarded as goods or commodities, a notion of which they demanded it be stripped. Like much else that is disguised or buried in the subconscious amid proletarian social issues, a significant factor persists: that a proletarian soul longs for its labour to be liberated from its designation as a commodity.

This can never happen, however, as long as the economy is run according to its own imperatives and all the activities of the state are made into a single economy, as is the ideal of many a socialist. Neither can it happen if the state tries unilaterally to make itself an economy. A healthy relationship only arises if the economy is allowed to develop within the confines of its own relative sphere of influence and when, as is fully unfolded in our natural organic bodies, a system containing inherent forces evolves in comparative independence, but which is then limited and improved by similarly independent adjoining systems or bodies. Though each may inflict damage, this is continually paralysed, disabled or neutralized by the adjoining system. All organic effectivity relies on this principle, and upon this must a potential recovery of the social organism's condition also rely.

I really do not mind how you define the economic sphere, nor that of the political state, nor how you think about them, but it is important to me that these two organisms have to coexist side by side, that one must evolve in relative independence and even, as far as its predisposition to harm necessarily has to develop, that the other system also has to evolve alongside it, incapacitating the worst effects of what would otherwise cause harm in the adjoining system. Such is the nature of living entities. It must also be acknowledged as the nature of a living social organism.

Only when the economic element self-governs within its own terms, which arise once the interpersonal political-legal sphere self-regulates—also according to its inherent lawfulness, which in turn arises from regulating interpersonal legal relations—and when each of these spheres self-governs independently, working adjacent to—and hence affecting—one another, only then will healthy societal life emerge. Social issues cannot be resolved with theories nor by passing laws, but only amid lively social living itself can forces of impetus be settled in immediate proximity: the economy alongside and interacting with a political-state domain, each acting within their self-supporting terms.

It is this which has been neglected for historical imperatives. What took place was, of course, necessary. No criticism is intended here, but instead a depiction of relationships. These must be established as a matter of necessity for progress in human life, both now and for the near future. It will become apparent that for the recovery of the social organism, economic life will have to be *associative*, will have to structure itself so that co-operatives, trades unions and so forth become a reality, while ridding itself of the obsolete notion that everything ought to be structured along old state-legislative lines. Any remaining features of the political state persisting in associations serving the economic sphere will have to be sloughed off. They will have to become associations serving the economy alone, bodies relying on the relationships people inevitably form within economic commerce, be it through reliance on the natural resources that are the foundations of the economy or on the need to utilize one raw material or another in bringing products into circulation, establishing the right relation between producing, trading and so on. The very complexity of life today causes a whole system of associated enterprises and coalitions involved in the natural foundations of the economy to be created among people. Such associations and coalitions are based on an understanding of the way in which raw materials are utilized and the manner in which they are channelled in the form of products to the consumer. Complexity of this kind demands the formation of a system of associations. They will be created out of the very connection between human being and commercial forces *themselves.* From this will ensue the oft-recurring real-life tendency for economies to exploit human beings.

Political processes ought to operate alongside the economy. In contradistinction to the economy—which needs to be associatively based—politics are to be based on democratic principles because state activity encompasses the relationships between human beings, including everything uniting people's interests. What in commerce relies on the economic value of goods, ought in the state to be principally based on statutory public law, which establishes in law—or which institutes the laws determining—the relationships between individuals. All that evolves from the economic sphere will then have to be limited, mutually restricted in dynamic reciprocity. Early signs of this can already be found but radical social insight still has to gain traction. Above all, mechanisms will have to be developed whereby people are protected from the economy—orientated as it is towards utility—so that their labour is itself not exploited.

Just as price-setting and adding value is fundamental among commercial bodies, so the elaboration of concretely specific laws and rights regulates life between people and is the essential feature of state-political actuality. As far as feelings about public rights are concerned, can one claim that they have achieved any real clarity? You can repeatedly ask those supposedly in the know, those who have pondered and researched the subject long and hard, what actually constitutes the basics of law, of the legislation always cropping up in concrete form. You gain, for instance, a sense of existing difficulties if you look into the issue underlying my late friend Ludwig Laistner's[20] doctoral thesis 'The Right to Sentence'. This can itself become the question: What constitutes concrete criminal law in human society?

Much can be tried when attempting to understand the impact of law. Particularly nowadays, when rights are discussed so widely and from so many perspectives, there is a perennial wish to access the essential nature of rights and jurisdiction. When trying to fathom what actually underpins law itself in a concrete sense, you encounter facts such as that property law is also legislatively based; land tenure is based on the exclusive right to own a plot of land or suchlike for one's sole use and activities to the exclusion of others, this being the object of the political arm of the social organism and, as many cannot but conclude, this ultimately goes back to power. Others maintain that it goes back to an archetypal human feeling. It is all too easy—when you come right down to tackling the issue—to arrive at empty formulas. Without going into an extensive rationale—which would take hours—I would just like to say that the law, that legislature and jurisprudence, establishes particular relationships, binding human beings to some object, process, series of proceedings or similar, to the preclusion of other human beings. How is it, then, that the feeling or perception may arise that some individual or nation has a right to what you have in your own sights? You arrive at the inescapable point—however hard you may struggle—of reflecting that, in public life, legal rights ensure the existence of preconditions which allow for someone to carry out some activity or process or series of proceedings which are more likely to benefit humanity as a whole than for any other reason. As soon as you have the impression that a person's relationship to a particular thing or process is an expression primarily of its benefit to humanity as a whole—as opposed to someone else's purposes or relationships—you can assign to the former the right to engage in that activity. This will be basically what incentivizes human sentiment when great legal-judicial issues of international coexistence arise, that is, become actual. Jurisdiction over territory will in future have to be awarded to the nation most able to offer safe, productive benefit to humanity as a whole.

You then come to what permeates and pervades a democratic state, what informs initiatives tasked with orientating life between people, be it by way of workers' or other insurance instituted to mitigate economic harm. In this respect, life itself has to be the underlying basis for the law, as just mentioned. An understanding—but not the sort of abstract generalities that usually define the law—an understanding of the real efficacy of the law in every specific case is what has to be inaugurated with a view to creating a healthy society right across humanity. This domain of the law, this political state—in its restricted sense—this second element in a healthy social organism, will indeed become that central juncture—if I may put it like that—of contemporary social issues, will become real not by putting theoretical opinion, principles or programmes into practice but by being the point in immediate, real life which I earlier described in terms of contemporary workers' demands: that human labour be divested of its commodity status.

For this to happen, it is also essential to understand—I'd say vital to grasp from bedrock upwards—what part human labour plays in life as a whole and in the structure of society. Again, it would take hours were I to elaborate in detail a single basic social law around human labour. I believe that anyone with a reasonable grasp of lived actuality will intuitively and instinctively understand what I am about to say. I tried to draw attention to this fundamental social law[21] in an essay on social issues, which appeared at the turn of the century in my then journal, *Lucifer Gnosis*. Much was said—and continues to be said—on this subject, but sadly it falls on deaf ears. This law embodies the fact that nobody—in as much as they are participants in the societal body or organism—really works for him- or herself. Please take note: by belonging to the social organism, people do not work for themselves. Work carried out by individuals can never directly benefit them, neither can the material proceeds of that work, which can only be for the benefit of others. Hence, what others produce must benefit us. Implicit in this is no mere ethically-nurtured altruism but a simple social law. We cannot do otherwise—in the same way as our blood cannot be redirected—than engage with circulating human activity in such a way that our activity benefits others and, conversely, that the work of others benefits us; that our own activity never reverts to us in the form of a benefit.

However contradictory it may appear, if you examine the circulatory effect labour has in the social organism, you will find that what originates in one person benefits others, while the results of others' labour benefits the individual. As I say, however paradoxical it may seem, it is nevertheless true: you can as little live from the proceeds of your own work in society as consume yourself by way of nourishment.

Although this law is basically easy to understand, you might object: If I were a tailor[22] making clothes for others and, amongst these, I were to make myself a suit, then my labour would indeed have been for my own benefit! That is just an illusion, in the same way as it is always illusory if I believe that the benefits of my own work revert to me. By making myself a skirt, some trousers or whatever, I am not really working for myself but I put myself in a position of having to do more work for others. This is the unalloyed function of a law of human labour within society. Those opposing this law are working counter to the interests of the social organism as a whole. That is why it is to work to the detriment of the social organism if you continue to put into practice what has come about in recent history: that workers are expected to live on the proceeds of their own labour. This is no verity but a fallacy engendered amid social obfuscation; it is falsehood incarnate, and it pervades and damages economies. This can only be regularized once an economy evolve independently, while alongside it there also evolve politics and a restricted state. This latter constantly denies the economy the opportunity to channel human labour back to itself. Within the legal system a correct social understanding of labour is achieved where human labour is afforded its rightful function in the context of real life in the social sphere. The economy per se always has a tendency to exploit human labour. Legal-judicial activity must ensure that it always accords to labour its naturally altruistic nature. It is ever and again essential that what the economy wants to achieve through fallacy be continually seized back from it by means of specific new democratic legislation and public rights, thereby repeatedly wresting human labour from the jaws of the economy. In the same way as the digestive system has to function with the respiratory-circulatory system, absorbing what digestion embodies, likewise must what takes place in the economy work alongside—and in reciprocity with—processes in the legal system, otherwise neither system thrives. The legislative system—if its aim is to become the economist—only stultifies the economy. If the economy wants to take possession of the state, it destroys it, killing off the very existence of public legal rights.

This is what I wanted to add to previous lectures in pursuit of founding a tripartite or threefold social organism. Because leading bourgeois circles have to some extent become as if hypnotically fixated on the state, it has become something of a totemic idol to them. Attention has not been directed towards the essential differentiation of society into three constituent elements. That is how it has come about that the state and politics (in its limited sense) have also absorbed and subsumed spiritual-intellectual culture. In the same way as the circulation of goods in the economy depends on setting prices and adding value, and life within the political-social sphere is dependent on a system of legal rights, so is all intellectual culture based directly on the content of what is produced by it. Just think what an enormous difference there is between economic and spiritual life. In the economy everything depends on goods being moved on to most expedient use. If you combine anything of spiritual origin—be it education, training, art or anything else originating in cultural-spiritual-intellectual realms—with any concept of utility, it becomes completely absurd. It cannot be done. You cannot put what is of spiritual origin into the self-same category as circulating products. For instance, it is through doing this that the modern state has been enabled to forcibly subsume education, training and universities into its ambit, and this has become—in a very literal sense—an oppressive factor, an oppression. It ought to alert people to the need for spiritual culture to be freed and unshackled.

I have drawn attention elsewhere to the fact that within this spiritual sphere of the social organism ought to be included—though it will seem paradoxical to some—the practical delivery of private and criminal law. Oddly enough, even today there is a tendency not to appraise this correctly. The flawed psychology to which jurisprudence increasingly has recourse tends towards an as yet unrecognized principle—but a principle which it is vital to identify: that of incorporating the work of private and criminal law into the intellectual sphere of the social organism, an intellectual culture which should exist in relative independence from all the activities evolving in the limited political sphere in public rights legislation. Clearly, in a salutogenic society of the future, criminals, for example, will be subject to processes taking place in the second, political, sphere. Once charged, however, they will be tried by a judge whom they will face in an *individual* human capacity.

A subject such as this can probably only be evaluated in historical terms by someone such as I who, in speaking to you now, have for many years been able to observe an area over which it was extremely difficult to govern centrally yet where people, I might say, nevertheless and counter-intuitively, wanted a mandatory unitary state. This area was Austria. There you could see what would have happened if—extending beyond mere language areas—integrated legal jurisdiction had prevailed. If, despite language barriers, a Bohemian in a German area would then have been able to select a judge from the neighbouring Czech or Bohemian regions—or, alternatively, if a Bohemian resident could have selected any judge from a German area. You could see how beneficial this principle was in the efforts of what sadly only remained beginnings among some school associations. For those who experienced life in Austria, it remains something of a nightmare and it weighs on the soul that this Columbus' Egg has not been, as it were, cracked. Free choice of judge, active co-operation between plaintiff, judge and defendant, instead of judges acting on behalf of a centralized political state, which could only be decisive in pursuing and delivering criminals—or in carrying out subsequent verdicts—but not in terms of legislative jurisprudence itself.

However contradictory this may seem, the relationship between individual and magistrate in private and criminal law must be incorporated into a free spiritual sphere. I referred to this the day before yesterday: that external administration and choice of personnel within this spiritual culture must not be subject to the state. To those who understand modern conditions it will also be obvious that the inmost living core of science, art and everything of a spiritual-intellectual, academic or cultural nature will come to depend on something upon which it would not be permitted to depend were this spiritual element allowed to evolve in relative independence alongside both the other spheres. It may still seem paradoxical to some people if I sum up by saying that each of these three areas needs to exercise a certain sovereignty over its own sphere of influence, have its own system of representation and delegation as well as a legislature grown out of its own circumstances: out of associative relationships in the economy. In other words to exercise control over—and laws within—their respective autonomous spheres. Originating among the population of each sphere, a specific social sphere for state politics itself will evolve democratically, in which relationships between people, towards the economy and towards spiritual culture will be settled, without state laws intervening in both other spheres. Likewise, stemming from forces active in spiritual culture, intellectual, academic activity will also structure and manage itself. Spiritual culture will be liberated to a far greater extent in modern life than was the case in times gone by when the sole spiritual element to affect many people consisted of religious activity, out of which in turn schools and universities evolved.

Admittedly, the state had to intervene in relegating outmoded religious tropes, removing from them their traditional but obsolete purview. Independent spiritual culture now has to evolve out of contemporary life itself. It is precisely to this end that spiritual-scientific objectives, underlying as they do these societal observations, have to lay claim, because they acknowledge that the sum of all productive spiritual culture—including everything advanced by technical thinking and technological innovation—can only develop in a way that really benefits humankind if it evolves out of a truly self-supporting and buoyant spirituality that is independent of the other two spheres of society. The spirit will only rightly derive its impetus towards human creativity once this spiritual culture acquires largely independent status. You can be as inventive as you like in aimless imaginings, theorizing and daydreaming—including, to my mind, what has so remarkably been occurring in certain technologies and sciences in respect of their methods—but the idea that is so genuinely productive that it serves true human progress and its deliverance, this idea can only be conceived within a self-determining, self-sustaining spiritual culture.

Today we are still so far from what I am proposing and intending, and from what needs to be understood as vital if social issues are to be put on a salutary basis, that some have reacted, when encountering this threefold rationale, claiming that it just recalls the ancient Platonic concept[23] of tripartitioning the body social into three echelons: rulers (philosopher-kings and guardians) auxiliaries (warriors, defenders) and producers (farmers, artisans and labourers). No, ours is no reinstatement of Plato's concept of tripartition but is in some respects its radical converse. And this is the whole point. Because between what was platonically conceived as something to be lauded for ancient Greece and subsequent times and what is here proposed for the restorative benefit of society lies the great crisis and incision into human existence which took place around the fifteenth century. In Plato's time the division of society was stratification by status or rank. The construction of which I am here speaking is not an apportionment among a population but a distribution among society such that a person could potentially belong to all three spheres with their attendant activities yet, inasmuch as the social organism will be structured, they are not in a position to cause harm to any other sphere, not even—as is the case in many a contemporary parliament—if they are both, say, a landowner and a member of a given political party. It is still possible today for a person to appoint representation of their interests through some association, committee or other so that an economic interest may be represented in a judicial context. Last time, I gave an example of one such economic interest being advocated and an entire state's legislative sphere being pervaded to societal detriment. This would be impossible here. Yet what I describe as threefold in a healthy society is a social entity, as it were, separate from the human person. People become self-reliant and divested of any traits reminiscent of being a slave of the social organism precisely because it embodies an *absence* of human classes, echelons and strata while instead society is itself structured. This shows that the thinking underlying it fully accords with reality and is far removed from anything resembling the zealous fantasizing I also termed swarm-raving a couple of days ago.

Zealotry of this sort can appear in the most varied quarters and is just as likely to be found in bourgeois as among social democrat circles. It takes hold of people wherever they repeatedly fail to develop the first notion as to what the social organism can itself achieve when it is healthy. Ever and again does society labour under the illusion that—through some programme or other—it can instantly become an organism capable of bringing about happiness among people, or providing at least something approaching contentment. This cannot be attained overnight. What *can* be achieved, however, is a viable organism capable of life, one containing vital forces for living. When incarnated in an organism of this kind, when inhabiting it, human beings find happiness from quite different substrata. It then has altogether differently grounded underpinnings. But these foundations have to be freed from their current constraints. They will only be liberated once they are established in a viable organism. Much as a soul can evolve within a genuinely viable physical structure and exist in resultant mutuality, likewise can populations inhabit a viable social structure in contentment, be happy, willing and aware in their work. This is the aim in restoring the social organism to health.

Even a cursory glance at what we have been experiencing in these catastrophic times will suffice, I would say—both from an international as well as a wider historical perspective—to confirm that the three elements I have been trying to introduce here are essential for the lives of present-day humanity, as also for the lives of those in the foreseeable future. I would like to suggest that the chaotic amalgamation, intermingling and entangling of these three elements—which now need disentangling—reached its zenith before the terrible cataclysm they call war engulfed the world. Much of what has contributed to the original causes of this martial catastrophe can, in all truth, be laid at the door of precisely these three elements not operating in parallel and in relative autonomous harmony. You need only look at a few symptoms. Everyone's attention had been directed towards the war apparently originating in relations between Austria and the Balkans, namely with Serbia. Those privy to Austrian relations over the last decades knew how to assess economic relations between Austria and the European South-East, how they were playing out abnormally and were enmeshed in alliances—which should have developed in parallel and comparative independence—with purely political elements; and how, due to being thus amalgamated, purely political groups were suddenly required to make decisions on matters deeply rooted in economics, through which a major falsehood was implanted into reality which subsequently exploded.

How different things could have been—I can only hint at this now, near the end of today's lecture—had threefolding been in place between neighbouring states. If across borders the relationship could have been purely political, based on democracy and separated from the other spheres, as would apply to other governmental fields. Had economic and spiritual elements likewise worked independently across borders as corrective and harmonizing forces, there would have been widespread concord and a confluence of interests between state—so-called state—systems such that they would have continually been self-correcting among themselves, and no unilateral eruptions could then have ensued. Beneficial cross-border threefolding would also create harmony-generating international relations between populations.

And then again, how did humanity as a whole view Germany's declarations of war, at least outwardly? Those inducted into those matters know how this calamity came about. During those baleful days of July and August it was widely alleged that politics—along with the actual conduct of war and military affairs—had collapsed. Yet politics and military matters are effectively synonymous. They cannot be separated without further ado. They can only develop beneficially when they are effective within a unified state structure, a social organism encompassing three spheres. Otherwise politics will—at least within that one sphere—necessarily be obliged to assume a unified character. At a given moment, this will result either in military or non-military consequences. Because what is homogeneous in nature—though confounded and admixed with other systems through human error—cannot in practice bring about mutual, reciprocal modification. Out of terrifyingly fear-filled conditions in Berlin—in the dying days of July and those first days of August—the enforced combination into a single system of all that should have been kept separate came about. It was forced together as the responsibility of a single authority, something for which a cohesive system for the benefit of all humankind should never be allowed to be responsible. Concrete circumstances will be particularly instructive once they have been freely researched, without restriction or prejudice. Oh, what a heap of nonsense has been uttered, particularly on the subjects of politics and military administration! So much rubbish has been spouted over the past four and a half years! I will mention just one thing. Because policies and tactics inherent in an indivisible sphere of the social organism can only there be effective, when strategy is obliged to manage itself alone, politics can never beneficially influence that strategy. It has been reiterated time and time again in the manner of Clausewitz:[24] 'Waging war is an extension of politics by other means.' I do not wish to respond critically to this dictum inasmuch as it is embedded in the entire martial controversy. But the way in which those gents—ladies likewise—repeatedly used that phrase makes as much sense as if one were to claim: 'Divorce is an extension of marriage by other means.'

Nonsense of this kind originates widely in unnatural thinking which has in turn naturally failed to get to grips with real circumstances. Once you look into matters impartially, it becomes apparent how differently all this could have turned out. Obviously, what happened was historically necessary, and what needs to be expressed will be valid as an impetus for the future, but one can say hypothetically how different a course everything would have taken had the structure of European international relations been instigated on principles of social threefolding. People will say: What happened came about due to situations involving alliances. But such alliances could never have come about had social threefolding been activated. An end to alliances such as those which led to the calamities of the last four and a half years is possible where people are aligned with the healthful threefolding of the social organism.

What I am here setting out is entirely thought through in line with reality, is thoroughly grounded in reality. That is why, while making efforts among relevant authorities during those awful years, I have always drawn attention to threefolding in a form suited to the times. What constitutes reality changes from day to day and it could well be the case that, if circumstances changed again, I would need to speak differently about a given situation. I said to those people: What is being proposed here is not some programme nor some ideal but is a result of observing what is *willing* to become a reality in the next ten or twenty years in Central and Eastern Europe—in Europe as a whole. You have a choice as to whether you wish to deploy reason today or face revolution and cataclysm tomorrow.

This has already started and will manifest in yet other ways. Today, however, I wish to reiterate what I have said in this regard on other occasions. I have always said: Those Utopians and theorists whose thinking is not grounded in reality but rather on certain abstract imperatives, partisan motivations or suchlike have a vested interest in seeing that directives set out in their programmes be carried out in every last detail. I said at the time that such are not my concerns with the issues I am here to represent—that is what I said at the time. It could be, I said—and I still say it today—that no stone remains standing of the model I am representing. Because it is not a matter of implementing some contrivance but ultimately of getting to grips with reality. Then, while grappling with reality, you will discover what the next steps ought to be. On further implementing it, it may turn out that the projected models need to be revised. The point—if you are no Utopian nor a swarming zealot—is not in literally carrying out directives but in really making a start somewhere. And I want to indicate one such 'somewhere' where a start has to be made today, before it is too late and before human instincts are unleashed on such a scale that—possibly for decades to come—comprehension and communication between people may no longer be possible.

That is why, in conclusion, let me give voice to something which does not strictly belong within this lecture. I do also think that anyone who today feels themselves to be connected at a soul level with social issues not only has an obligation to raise those issues but—by all available means—to secure their contemporaries' understanding of them. Because generating shared social understanding is something we can all do, for a start. So much has been ruined and bedevilled across the world due to myopic thinking—as described recently—being summoned into the world instead of proper, timely thinking. I must therefore greet with a certain satisfaction the fact that it has become possible—within a fairly short space of time, despite the trials of the present situation—to put into practice aspects of what I am speaking about. Those individuals who had in some way been fired, if I may put it thus, by the view of societal reality here presented have committed to working towards an understanding of that society, whose current misfortunes can at least be its greatest teacher. However, I'd consider it an exceptional delight if in this Swiss territory—where the chance of some wholly calm objectivity exists—that, just because of this calm objectivity, an even deeper reciprocal understanding of society were to arise among people to the end that they understood the need to *do* something along the lines of what is suggested in the four lectures given to date. Nevertheless, amid the pain we can feel—indeed compounding that pain—about the course some events have taken and the fate some sectors of humankind are suffering, there is a certain satisfaction in knowing that misfortune has after all been instructive for some. So it was possible—forgive me for digressing, but it is vital not to be abstract but concretely practical when discussing social issues—for me to frame an appeal[25] into which, in succinct form, I have incorporated much of what I have been elaborating here. This appeal is intended to be effective worldwide but has so far gained access to the hearts only of those in Germany and German-speaking Austria who have been so sorely tested by adversity and who have to some extent learnt from it. In that appeal or petition I attempt to articulate what was then being founded as the German Empire, which occurred at a time when contemporary humanity's evolutionary potential was most urgently calling for just such a refounding and transition to new social tasks. Minor aspects had in fact been widely embraced; but precisely what should have featured uppermost in this Empire in order to give to its framework relevant content based on contemporary evolutionary forces—content aligned with threefolding—this they were unable to envisage. That is how the rest of the world came to take its lead from Central Europe. How could the rest of the world understand the justification for the specifics of this Empire's founding if from it there ensued nothing to demonstrate the compelling attractions of such an Empire within international developments?

That is why I believed, if what I may call a properly programmed plan—which, as you know from what has been said, is no theoretical programme but congruence with reality—that is why I believed I could articulate a global appeal to take up a task which could in future evolve out of European humanity, faced as it is with the need to build anew from the ground upwards. It was at least gratifying to experience that, by yesterday midday, this petition had attracted more signatures in Germany than that erstwhile call from those ninety-nine intellectuals of unhappy memory. Over a hundred of those signatures came from Germany and, by yesterday, over sixty names from German-speaking Austria. I mention this because I want to speak on the basis of reality and thereby draw your attention to the fact that I am not alone in thinking onward social progression is essential and, when it comes to it, this will be substantiated by bringing about reciprocal social relationships.

Initially, more work will need to be done by way of properly informing and enlightening society. Because that is obviously the first thing to do. Much of humanity and the developed world is faced with the need to really look social issues in the eye. In doing so they will have to solve a problem. Let me in conclusion say something most extremely uncomfortable for *habitual* thinking. Many people still concede that making changes to infrastructure and transforming social structures is crucial. Hasn't the entire spirit of the lectures I have been afforded the liberty of giving proved that something else is also needed? Though proletarian leaders of Marxist leaning continually persist in emphasizing the truth of the Marxist maxim that 'Philosophers[26] have interpreted and explained the world,' it's not just a matter of *explaining* the world in terms of thinking, but of actually *transforming* it. Despite the acutely pressing demands of the times, this axiom only represents a half-truth, possibly not even a quarter-truth. What is needed is not just thought being applied to changing structures, but it is vital to *change the thoughts themselves.* A healthy social organism will only be capable of evolving out of newly transformed, renovated thinking. People quite like rearranging structures but are far less fond of radically modifying their thinking. But that is imperative. Until you realize that, you will be unable to orientate yourselves, unable to collaborate in restoring society to health.

Social challenges have long been knocking at our doors as the most important of human considerations in need of resolution. They have now come home to roost in humanity's lodgings. They can no longer be shown the door because this theme is an enchantress, as regards evolution, working not only on the external fabric of humanity but confronting it with the need to transform its thinking, or else to heap ever more tragedies onto the disasters already at hand.

In saying this, I am expressing what is required, what has to be made a reality, if it is not to be too late as regards instincts—as mentioned—taking on forms and extents that make it impossible for understanding to come about between differing echelons of society. We can only effect the healing of society once we establish a social organism based on innovation—something we anticipate—and on salutogenic principles—for which we cherish hope. To this end we must stop relying on antiquated thinking and instead boldly and energetically resolve to use our strength to turn to fresh thinking for the onward progress of humanity. Because opportunities in life for new generations will only blossom if founded on new thinking. You will have to think about social challenges as having grown out of modern living conditions. But you will be mistaken if you imagine you can somehow solve them instantly. Socialism is no sort of solution, nor even a real attempt at resolving matters. No, present life and that of humanity into the future has raised these social concerns. They will always exist and they will always have to be resolved within any society. Life for future humanity will always contain its quota of social trials, which successive generations will each have to solve anew in innovative ways. Now that it has been raised, this social challenge will forever reproach us and shake the fabric of human thinking and willing. Let us turn to it wholeheartedly, with all our souls, otherwise it will turn on us, not for our good but for our undoing.

Lecture 5

Zurich Student Union, 25 February 1919

Social will as a basis for a new scientific system

This title has been requested as the subject of today's lecture. I am not sure what motivated the choice of this particular theme but, when its challenge reached me, I thought it an exceptionally felicitous choice because it does indeed set the tone for what strikes me as needful in the face of everything the social movement has hauled into the present. This is something which actually speaks far more eloquently than what have been preparatory discussions and debates around social issues over past decades.

The evolution of this social movement can be traced over long periods and into the present, and it is noticeable, in relation to the social will increasingly being expressed in favour of the wishes of one faction or another, that something has crept in, has insinuated itself into the social will and attitudes of recent times. This something may appear like a shroud of superstition more redolent of medieval times, an emergent shibboleth like that encountered when you read or watch the second part of Goethe's *Faust*. This is the scene where Goethe sets Wagner to preparing his Homunculus, a small quasi-humanoid he aims to make fully human. Here, Goethe shows us the medieval superstition which thought it could produce something living out of a theoretical composite of stolid, desiccated facts synthesized by human reason. Goethe was particularly taken with the impossibility of making something living out of abstractions drawn from external life. Medieval thinking of this sort does not govern present thinking as such. But it seems to me that a metamorphosis of that superstition still haunts the motivations and instincts of our contemporaries, among whom are many who want to subscribe to social action. Observing the evolution and emergence of societal life throughout human history and into the present, people think up all sorts of principles or ground rules on the basis of which people are expected to proceed or—as can be heard in some quarters—which are themselves wanting to self-actuate. They think they can—with the same abstract notions tried on the Homunculus—create something we are calling a social organism.

I might say that modern humanity's subconscious is indeed motivated towards just such a body social. You just have to be clear about the following to understand that. Human social life per se is, of course, nothing new but it now manifests in a different form. The social structure of society has, until recent times, been determined by human instincts and subconscious impulsions. This is the salient point in recently emergent forces: that humanity can no longer just remain static amid instinctual willing but is challenged, by the nature of evolution itself, to equip itself to give shape to social structures. If you want to equip yourself with conscious will, you need, as a foundation, thinking capable of taking on reality, not thoughts abstracted from reality. You need thinking that is capable of acquainting your own will with forces pre-existing in natural phenomena and universal imperatives themselves. This involves becoming familiar with the creative forces of natural existence.

That is something whole swathes of humanity still have to learn. They will have to learn to think that they cannot proceed if they are still asking: what needs to happen for us to replace living conditions many feel to be unbearable with a viable social structure? You cannot proceed from that premise. You cannot imagine to any real extent what their social ills might be. You can only direct your best intentions to finding out how people themselves—living as they do in mutual relationships—might create the reciprocal harmony required to develop that changed social structure.

It seems to me, on the basis of many years' study of social phenomena, that you need to view the fundamentals of this social challenge—which today tend to be seen as constituting a single issue—in terms of three sectors, in other words, in a threefold way. Firstly as a spiritual-cultural issue, secondly as a legal matter and thirdly as one of the economy. What has emerged in the capitalist economy of modern times has of late done so on a basis of technology, which has in turn drawn our attention—as if by hypnotic fixation—exclusively towards the economy, diverting it away from considering the other two components of society: legislative-rights and spiritual-intellectual culture.

I may be allowed to address the spiritual issue first, not—as some might think—because I consider the spiritual angle to be especially close to me subjectively, but because I am of the view—though it tends to be proletarian-leaning thinkers who reject this—that in spiritual-intellectual culture I recognize something that can contribute positively to social issues, especially for those who are in touch with reality. That is why the spiritual sphere is being dealt with first. To understand this you have to view the true spirit and stature of the individuals who are moved by present social movements. You have to try to identify the will motivating those in socialist-orientated circles; you need primarily to identify the source of their impulses of will.

You see, as contemporary life has emerged on the back of technology and capitalism, leading sectors of society—those so-called ruling or leading classes, those pre-eminent echelons—have distanced themselves ever further from the proletarianism evolving in diverse areas. Those in the know will not deny that between proletarian will and non-proletarian life there is a gulf, a chasm, which can hardly be bridged unless you at least try not to enlist outdated thinking and obsolete impulsions of will, but become active in society with fresh thinking and new initiative of will. The belief among proletarians themselves has increased over time that socially disadvantaged people can hope for nothing from presently ruling classes and, as matters stand, this belief cannot be seen as entirely without foundation if they hope to build on their goodwill, ideas and so forth. If I may say so, a deep distrust has developed between societal echelons. This mistrust has arisen from deep substrata and has not until now emerged into consciousness, while continuing to exist subconsciously. From this it recently occurred that the working class extended towards the bourgeoisie one last great gesture of trust, and that—not through conviction but in the form of a feeling—this trust has been rejected and abused. You see, there is talk today of a proletarian world outlook. Many people, including some in leading positions, who believe they are expressing proletarian will in conceptual form, don't actually know what the origins are of that willing and thinking. Life's daily demands, which are live issues in the social movement, are in marked contrast with what even the proletariat themselves think about such social incentives.

If I am to summarize briefly what I mean in this regard, I would have to say: That is the nature of the way in which proletarian social culture has arisen. But within working people's feelings, within their social life and culture, a legacy of just such views and outlooks predominates as have resulted—at the decisive moment in their historical evolution—precisely from the bourgeoisie.

Observers of that decisive moment in recent history have to see it as existing within the context of scientific thinking's present state of development—and please note that I am not saying: natural science per se but the *thought tropes* current in present science—which has evolved from ancient spiritual impulses in such a way that scientific thinking no longer possesses the momentum, the same spiritual force of impact, that used to be inherent in the world outlooks of bygone times.

Those old world outlooks were embedded in broader motivating forces than are modern modes of scientific thinking. World conceptions of yore were capable of imparting to people motivating impulses by means of which—in the form of feelings and sensations—they could answer the question constantly stirring them, such as: *What am I* as a human being, *what am I* in relation to the world? Such force of psychic impact is not accorded modern scientific thinking. Obviously, as a result of historic imperatives—which are none the less historically fateful—older world views arraigned themselves in enmity against new scientific thought tropes at the decisive moment instead of enabling the confluence in friendship of their import for humans at a soul level. That is in fact how the following situation came about.

The machine age and the capitalist economic system tore a sector of humanity out of their lives' earlier contexts, out of contexts in which they had hitherto existed and into circumstances totally alien to their awareness of being human—to their sense of human dignity—where once there had been a connection between what an individual did and their personal standing in life. Just think of the affiliations among the crafts that were so prominent until the thirteenth century and how remnants of them persisted still later! It is from out of this context that large numbers were hurled at machinery, thrown into industrial economic systems. Here there are no remotely recognizable affinities with the means of production, no opportunity to create a relationship between human and actual activity. So it is precisely this aspect of being human—unaddressed and unnurtured by the machine age—which prompts the contemporary proletariat to ask: What am I worth as a human being? What is my true value?

This question can no longer be answered in terms of now superseded and meaningless living contexts. It can only be accessed from within each person, from that element which remains independent of outer circumstances. This group of people were left no alternative to what emerged in world history simultaneously with the machine age and the capitalist economic model: the resulting scientific mode of thinking.

The old system of classes had not been required to incorporate this scientific thinking into their beliefs and world outlooks. They only needed to make it their theoretical persuasion because what they invested in life was received tradition full of motives belonging to times long gone. Hence it was proletarians alone who, torn from all this, could commit to no concept of life bound up with world views predicated upon antiquated life contexts and who, precisely due to their external circumstances, were destined to make the new situation into their own intellectual content. However counter-intuitive it may sound, this is why the proletariat are in fact the original purely science-orientated sector.

To do justice to the momentous implications of this fact, it is not enough merely to have studied and thought about the working-class movement. You have to put yourself, as it were, into the shoes walking their destiny, into a situation of thinking *with* them; that is, thinking along the same lines as those who became the driving force of the working-class movement. You would then have felt clearly how what hailed from the past extended forward into the immediate social present.

Might you not reflect that it was bourgeois circles who took up scientific thinking most extensively? Just look at intellectual bourgeois circles, think of those who are overwhelmingly aligned—in their thinking and convictions—with science. And yet, as regards their feelings and their entire perception of life, they are nevertheless embedded in conditions not solely a product of scientific alignment. You can be a materialistic thinker, can consider yourself enlightened, be an atheist, can really commit in all honesty to these tenets, but you don't necessarily need to dissociate yourself, on a feeling level, from all those remnants of bygone life, which are not, after all, a product of scientific alignment but which originate in an age still fired by spiritual initiative, as just outlined.

A purely scientific alignment affects society in quite different ways. I am not saying *the sciences per se*, because obviously the scientific *tendency* also affected the less well educated or unskilled working proletariat. But its effects were very different when transposed onto the proletariat in the form of an ideological philosophy of life.

I'd like to illustrate this with an example. Many years ago I shared a lecture podium with Rosa Luxemburg,[27] now so tragically lost to us. She was speaking on the subject of 'Science and Workers'. I often remember how she drew the attention of that large audience in such a fiery manner to the fact that in reality all prejudice connected with social standing or personal rank among the old ruling classes was bound up with ideas innately involving spiritual world conceptions, as of old. The only thing that matters to the modern proletarian, she opined, is to hear how humans are not descended from divine angelic origins but how they once cavorted immodestly in trees, having evolved from animal substrata, from foundations which, if you follow their evolution honestly, must actually underlie the conviction that human equals human and that all previous disparities in rank hail from one prejudice or another. Here we are not looking at the interpretation but at the power of impact that such words have had on proletarian-minded sensitivities.

I had only that concept in mind when I said that today's proletariat is *scientifically* orientated in its entire world outlook. This science has failed to fulfil their sentience to the extent that it could positively answer the question 'What am I, in truth? What does it mean to be human in this world?' in a way that chimed with their feelings.

Where did the proletariat acquire this view? Where did the scientific tendency originate which they were sometimes obliged to absorb by dubious means? It is after all science. They appropriated this legacy from the bourgeoisie. It arose from old world concepts prevalent among the bourgeois middle classes at the pivotal point into the new capitalist machine age, when this new age had overwhelmed human beings.

The next thing you often hear, variously nuanced, is this: within the proletariat, spirituality and intellectual culture is now experienced as an *ideology*. You'll hear this most frequently when the underlying principles of the working-class outlook are being discussed: that art, religion, science, convention, rights and so on are nothing more than ideological mirror images of external material reality.

But this sense that all spiritual-cultural endeavour is ideology did not arise within the proletariat. They received it in the form of a legacy, a poisoned chalice, from the bourgeoisie. The last act of trust, that last great act of faith extended by the proletariat towards the bourgeoisie resulted in it having imbibed this sustenance for their spiritual-intellectual nourishment. Once the proletariat had been divested of its spiritual life, once it had been summoned by the machine away from all past contextual associations and installed in that social structure, it could only admire what had been developing in terms of human and global knowledge; it could only look aloft to what had evolved from the middle classes. It took on devoutness—I'd actually say dogma—and it absorbed ideology from the bourgeoisie. This didn't extend into actual belief but rather into the feeling of disappointment that inevitably arises when you cannot see what is spiritual as embodying a higher reality but only in terms of ideology. In the subconscious feelings of a large number of socialist movement leaders the sensation is not yet conscious but is powerfully felt: we have extended great trust towards middle-class civic society and we have inherited what ought to have endowed us with sustaining strength. The bourgeoisie has failed to deliver this and has only given us ideologies devoid of reality and incapable of sustaining life.

It can long be debated whether or not ideology really represents the underlying character of spiritual-intellectual culture. That is not at issue. But the crux of the matter is that spiritual life is felt by large swathes of humanity to be an ideology. If life is experienced as an ideology, sentience is stultified and remains empty, spiritual buoyancy is debilitated and what ensues has now indeed ensued: the feeling that social will has been stripped of its faith in evolving spirituality, the hope that an epicentre might emerge somewhere, some truly central hub from which healing and good could flow towards workers' views of the world and so forth; likewise in relation to an optimum structuring of the social movement. I'd even say that spiritual culture has brought a negative element into the evolution of contemporary proletarian humanity, while at the same time a positive element is increasing the yearning among that sector of humanity. They are demanding support at a soul level, yet they have been bequeathed only a soul-destroying legacy.

This is something that wafts and trickles silently throughout our entire social movement, something which cannot be grasped with concepts, but which both comprises and affects the structure of one societal movement and element—we will become acquainted with all three of these. As soon as you realize that this is the case, you can justifiably ask yourselves: How has this come about? How can it be remedied? Instead of will—social will—remaining paralysed, how can it be fired and reinvigorated? These questions need to be faced.

Now, an event occurred just when modern spirituality arrived at the critical point already mentioned. The circumstances of the pre-eminent classes of yesteryear were bound up with what we now term the state. People have often pointed out—due to time constraints I can't corroborate to what extent rightly or wrongly—that nowadays people believe that what they call the state has always existed in its present form. That is definitely not the case. What we call the state or nation today—and what Hegel, for example, equates with an expression of divinity itself—is basically just a product of thinking prevalent over the past four or five centuries. The social entities of earlier ages were quite different.

Take just one fact, take the recent fact that the erstwhile free schools and higher education establishments, which were founded quite independently of the state, have become a plethora of state institutions, such that the state has effectively become the custodian of humanity's spiritual, intellectual and cultural assets. That the state has appropriated this role is attributable to middle-class interests at the start of recent times. It was to the state that citizens grew habituated at a soul level and to which they became bound for all their needs. It is out of this relationship, this recent correlation between spiritual-cultural assets and the state, that the latter became the custodian of humankind's intellectual-spiritual trove and that it demanded of those approaching that warder that they define their very lives according to its imperatives.

If you delve a little deeper into the fabric of humanity's spiritual cache, you find not only that its external administration, the governance of universities, primary and other schools, has become state-controlled but even its spiritual-intellectual content has itself become state-run.

Admittedly, mathematics bears no state impress. But other branches of our intellectual life do bear its imprint and have of late been branded by the convergence of state interests with all that is of a spiritual or intellectual nature. This convergence is not without liability for our spiritual trove becoming an ideology. Spiritual-cultural abundance can only shoulder and preserve its innate integrity if it is able to self-govern on its own terms, having its own powers and if, on its own direct initiative, it can give to the state what is appropriate to the state without, crucially, being obliged to comply with state requirements or demands.

There may doubtless be many who see no fundamental social reality in what I have just said. Yet here again, you will see that the spirit governing reality can only do right by humanity if that spirit is separate from external state bodies and reliant only on itself. I know what objections can be raised, but that's beside the point. Here it is purely that, in order to flourish, spirit requires leave in perpetuity to act out of the free and direct initiative of the human individual.

Here we are approaching the true nature and conundrum of this societal component. The spiritual sphere is only viewed correctly—and its prerequisites understood—if elements overlapping or projecting into state structures are gradually withdrawn from state jurisdiction, enabling them to unfold their innately supportive cultural capacities independently, alongside the other societal spheres. In return—because its culture will then have been freed—it will be able to benefit society as a whole. If we are to talk in practical terms about this intellectual sphere, we would have to say: The progressive trend has to be towards the widest possible *disunion* or *decoupling* of the spiritual-intellectual sphere from the state. One segment in particular also needs to be extricated from the state. It may today seem contrary to claim that the relationship of a judge with individuals involved in criminal or civil law is primarily a *human* one—something recognized among some psychologists, albeit from a different perspective—and is such an *individually personal* association that judicial activity ought really to be included in the spiritual sphere. Also to be included in this sphere is everything of a religious-faith nature, all artistic endeavour, but also everything contingent upon civil and criminal law; the direction, again, has to be one of separation from the state, that is, de-nationalization.

Would anyone hearing of such radical measures immediately think of violent revolution? Even among socialists, people are gradually coming away from that thought. I too share the thought that de-nationalization cannot happen overnight. But I do think that humanity's social will can inhabit every single measure it takes—and this may need reviewing daily, as appropriate—and has to be orientated towards an eventual dissolution of the state-spiritual-culture nexus. You will be able to imagine what I have in mind in concrete terms.

We should view the state as being something with which the middle classes—while making themselves the leading societal echelon—are increasingly enamoured. The bourgeoisie has allowed the state not only to subsume spiritual culture but also the sphere which in recent evolution has as if engulfed the social organism wholesale: the economy. Insinuating economics into the state has long been under way in areas of commercial interest such as the postal system, railways and so forth, which have been nationalized. As a result, a superstitious attitude towards the state and state-leaning communities has arisen. A last remnant of this superstition is the belief harboured by socialist-inclined populations that salvation will only come in the form of collective governance of the entire economy. Here, too, a legacy of bourgeois thinking and attitudes has been appropriated.

Now we have placed spiritual culture on the one hand, economic activity on the other and, between them both, is the state.

You may ask yourselves: What remains for the state? We will soon see how economic activity cannot withstand being admixed and confused with the state. Perhaps we can gain a clearer view of this by bearing in mind what the middle classes actually found in the emerging modern state: they found a refuge for their legal rights.

Let's look at what legal rights actually are. I'm not only thinking of criminal law but also about civil or private law inasmuch as it doesn't involve individual, inter-personal relationships, and I'm also thinking of public law. Public law includes, for example, transactions and dealings concerning property ownership. And what exactly is property? Property ownership is just an expression of justification for possessing something for your sole use—and having permission to work on or process it—in your capacity as a person. Ownership has its roots in law. Everything we generally designate as external items has its roots in its relationship to human beings by way of law. Bourgeois classes and civic society had acquired rights such as these in times preceding our conception of a modern state, and found them to be best safeguarded by subsuming everything relating to vouchsafing those rights into the ambit of the state itself.

This is the route by which economies tended to be ever more closely drawn into state activity. The state pervades the structures of the economy with a number of laws and these rights are *in no way* to be included when evolving towards the future. Social will needs to evolve by educating itself to a point where it can differentiate accurately between everything of a *legal-rights* nature, of an inherently *spiritual* quality, and things specifically *economic* in function.

A modern social movement will make this especially vivid because ruling echelons have failed to include something in the legal-rights area of their modern state. Whilst they have extracted much from the economy—from the purely isolated economy—and incorporated it into the legal framework of the state, they have failed to incorporate the following into that framework: the labour of proletarian workers, which has been left within the cyclic round of economic processes.

It is this that has become deeply incised into the minds of proletarians and which was rationalized to them by Marx and his successors like this: there is always a market for labour, just as there is a market for merchandise. In the same way as goods are tendered on commodity markets and demand for them exists, you bring your labour—*the only resource you possess*—to the labour market and it is just deemed to be a commodity. It is bought, like a commodity, and exists within economic processes as a commodity.

With this we are approaching the true form of our second social challenge. This is expressed in that, issuing from a certain unconscious stratum of their sense of human dignity, today's working classes felt it to be intolerable that their labour was being bought and sold on commodity markets.

Admittedly, socialist thinkers claim theoretically: the fact that labour has been submitted to markets in the same way as other goods is attributable to objective laws operating within the economy itself. They are conscious of this. So, probably, are workers themselves. Yet something quite different dominates subconsciously: a perpetuation of bygone issues of slavery and serfdom. At this subconscious level, you see how individual human beings in their entirety were put onto labour markets to be bought and sold as goods i.e. slaves, and that subsequently a slightly smaller proportion of a person was enslaved and how what still persists is workers' labour. In this respect, however, they are wholly submitting to the economic process. And this is experienced as insufferable and beneath their dignity.

Following from this is today's second challenge: decommodifying labour.

I know that today large numbers of people wonder how this can be achieved. How else can an economy be operated than by paying labour forces? In asking this, you are already in effect buying their labour! You would only need to counter that even Plato and

Aristotle assumed an obvious need for slavery. So today's thinkers may be forgiven for considering it unavoidably necessary to market and monetize labour.

You cannot always anticipate what may turn out to be the reality of the near future. But today you do need to ask: By which means can labour be divested or stripped of its commodity status? This can only be achieved by elevating it into the sphere of the purely constitutional state, that is, the state from which, on the one hand, a spiritual sphere has been separated out—as described—and, on the other, a state from which everything just described as belonging to economic processes has also been removed. If we then structure the entire social organism—or think of it as thus structured—into these three constituent parts: independent spiritual culture, legal and economic spheres respectively, then instead of a Faustian Homunculus we will have a genuine human in the economic sphere. Then, too, our spiritual mind's eye will be focused on a genuinely viable model for societal living and not on some synthetic agglomeration of a social organism.

I really don't want to play the game of analogies between biology and sociology—that is the very last thing I want to do—nor do I want to fall into the errors of Schaeffle or Meray[28] in his 'World Mutation'. I want to avoid all that, but that's not the point. What is apposite is to observe how, within each natural human body, three independently coexisting systems are active in parallel. I outlined this by way of a scientific sketch in my book *Riddles of the Soul.* Similarly, three independent systems are applicable to the body social: spiritual-cultural sphere, legal-judicial system with that of public law—as I said, civil private- and criminal law would not be included—and then the economy itself.

However, when the regulatory state and the laws governing it are positioned between spiritual and economic spheres, then something compatible with real life will have been integrated into society as a whole, much as in the human being where you find the relatively self-sufficient systems of circulation, lung-and-heart existing between cerebral-brain and metabolic-digestive systems. Then again, once the state is on its own turf, as it were, and fully elaborated outside the purely economic—think of governance, democratic regulation of this legal-rights field—and when each person has equal claim on their rights and governance, which only regulates the relationship between individuals on this particular turf, then incorporating labour into the economic process will have become something quite different from the present situation.

So you see that I'm not just giving you some precept or theory. It can be achieved in this way if you want to strip labour of its commodity status. But I am saying: How should people initially relate to reorganizing the body social so that, with their actions, with their thinking, with their will, something capable of life is the result? I won't prescribe some panacea but I am just describing how human society would need to be organized so that their healthy social *will* results in an abiding, enduring social organism capable of—and congruent with—life itself. I want to replace theoretical thinking with thinking that is, as it were, on closely familiar terms with reality. What might result if—quite separately from economic activity, under employment legislation and on territory governed relatively exclusively by itself—if on territory such as this, people dealt with employment law purely on the basis of what stems from human substrata, and if, on that basis, laws were to be made? Then something would result that would affect the economy similarly to the way in which nature now provides the foundations for its processes. These natural foundations of the economy can be seen and studied when clearly in our sights. They determine the economic process such that human beings are deprived of their own contribution to those very processes. You just need to take note of what is noticeable, don't you?

Just suppose—I will give an extreme example—that in certain countries, albeit far from here, a banana is an extraordinarily significant thing. Yet the labour involved in getting the banana to its place of consumption is minimal at its origin in comparison with that required, let's say in our European context, for wheat to be transported to its consumers' destination. The labour which renders the banana consumer-ready in comparison with wheat has a ratio of—or even above—roughly one to a hundred. So, a hundred times more labour is involved in conveying wheat to consumers than is the case for bananas. There could be many more examples from the economy to illustrate the great differentials that exist in the management of commerce. These are independent of what humans themselves bring to the process: they lie in soil productivity and other factors and are inserted into the economy as constants that are independent of producers themselves. That is one aspect.

Now think of the labour-and-legal-rights area existing quite separately on one side, opposite that economic activity. Once there is no economic interest in the setting of working hours, in the deployment of work forces independently playing into purely inter-human matters, then something will result that is independent of the economy, just as from the opposite side we see factors originating in its natural foundations.

When setting prices[29] one is guided by the market value of a commodity and by the way in which natural factors affect this. If society is to be life-compatible in future, a production model will have to be taken into account and a goods circulation template created. If this template is not to determine rates of pay, working hours, workers' rights within employment law in general, then—independently of the product cycle and commodities markets and within the purview of state-rights legislation—working hours or conditions are set purely according to human needs and their perspectives, then it will be the case that a given product costs as much as has been required for its manufacture in terms of time and specific labour, yet which is determined by life independently from the economy. For instance, whereas today the economy unilaterally dictates working conditions such that the price of a product often has to determine these conditions, hours and so on within a local economy, the very opposite will be the case once a properly structured social organism is inaugurated.

Today these measures can only be suggested. Yet you see that they originate in social intentions very different from those which have landed us in such a parlous position among world events. They stem from social will which has not originated in some hare-brained scheme involving charitable, non-profit thinking, nor does it prescribe how this or that has to be carried out. Neither does this thinking stem from concepts about reality of a kind that cannot see the light of day while people are still randomly placed across the social organism. Once they are wholesomely embedded within society, they will determine matters correctly and work constructively.

You only need to have experienced the ways in which other socially-intentioned people organize matters in real life, for instance in that failed country, Austria. It had been a state but as a state comprised not only a legislative rights area but an economy which was, to an extreme degree, furthering the interests of groups of individuals. Just think how the old Austrian parliament functioned until the end of the 1890s! It was due to what was represented in this parliament that everything leading to the catastrophic First World War ensued. This government consisted of four committees or curia: a Chamber of Commerce, one made up of largescale landowners, one consisting of selected Town Councils, markets and industrial magnates, and an immovably ensconced economic group. This economic group was not representing, on the ground, any economic assembly yet their interests determined the state's political system, in other words, public-rights legislation was being defined by that group's interests. Just as it is by definition impossible for a secular, denominationally-minded party—such as existed in the last German Reichstag or Imperial Parliament—to exist while influencing legal institutions of the state, it is equally impossible for a society disposed to allow interested parties to determine rights legislation to be capable of supporting genuine life. The legislative system has to evolve in distinct separation, and to concern itself only with inter-personal matters which, as far as I'm concerned, is an absolutely democratic process. Then this legal framework will legislate as befits a threefold organism: on the one hand regulating economic activity and on the other its natural foundations.

In this economic sphere, which would now include representatives of the most varied branches of industry, purely economic factors and interests would pertain. The social organism would then contain—if I may express it in terms that were routine at the time—three classifications or constituents, each with its own legislative process and governance. I'd like to suggest they relate to each other like sovereign states, reckoning with each other even while somewhat intermingling. That may seem complex and uncomfortable to some but it represents the one and only healthy future-proof model that will render society competent in supporting real life. Because the economy itself will only be defined by its factors if on the ground purely economic interests are active; and these will only be determinable by the relationship necessary between production and consumption. This relationship between production and consumption can only be achieved on an *associative, co-operative* basis, as it could have evolved from a trades union or collective context. However, nowadays trades unions and other associative collectives are still heavily imprinted with those state features out of which they grew. They need to grow towards the economy and to evolve as bodies serving solely that economy for society to progress healthily.

I know that what I am saying may sound extremely radical to some. Be that as it may, that's neither here nor there. The actual point is that society becomes capable of supporting real life and that people, by making a start at emerging from old instinctive societal norms towards a more conscious social life, become enthused by initiative stemming from insight into our entire existence as a society. It is considered ignorant not to know your multiplication tables and thought uneducated not to know some basic facts. Yet you are not deemed an ignoramus if you have no social awareness or if you lounge around, comatose, within the social organism. That has to change totally in future! Things will be different once people are equipped with even the most basic ability in *social willing*, exactly as a degree of facility is expected with multiplication tables. Everyone needs to know what three times three is. In future it will be no less fundamental to know how interest on capital relates to the basic pension, to pick an example from current life. This will be no harder than three times three. Yet knowledge such as that will provide a basis for being healthily grounded in society, that is, in a healthier societal existence, something for which it is well worth aiming.

What I have been talking about is already nascent in human consciousness. You just need to have a nose for the potential that is struggling to manifest and be structured anew in daily life.

Just think back to the three great ideals of the French Revolution: Freedom, Equality and Fraternity. Those following what these ideas have wrought in the minds of humans and how they have fared over time will know how often people have struggled logically with the inherent contradictions that exist between freedom—intuitively pointing towards the unique individual and indicative of personal initiative on the one hand—and the equality implicit in implementing the centralizing forces of the state in society. It doesn‘t work. Yet a search for this confusing paradox has emerged in recent times. That today's capitalism cannot yet grasp the concept of a threefold social organism is a result of the notion of a totally centralized state.

If you consider the willed intentions expressed in the three ideals of freedom, equality and fraternity, it can easily be conceived of today from the perspective of a tripartite social organism. The first element you encounter is a spiritual or intellectual culture, which must be suffused with the principle and impetus of freedom. Everything has to be based on the free initiative of the individual and will, when successful, be at its most fruitful when thus based.

As regards state legislature—that state body which governs between the spiritual and economic spheres, indeed politics as such—the equality existing between individual human beings is what must suffuse everything.

With regard to the economy: here fraternity alone must be the guiding principle: socially co-experiencing all external and internal life, each human being through all the others.

Within the economy, interest alone can be the guiding factor. This interest brings a particular feature of the economy to the fore. Towards what is basically everything streamlined? To which outcome does everything in the economy flow? Its course is such that the products manufactured by a given industrial process have to be—to the highest, most appropriate degree—useable or consumable. I'm talking about consumption or use in a limited sense, one from which any spiritual trait is absent. Human labour, for instance, can be used. However, contemporary human beings feel that their labour should not simply be used nor exploited. In the same way that they secure an interest through their labour, they also need to acquire an interest in products of spiritual culture through their leisure, through their peaceable capacity to absorb what is culturally spiritual. The economy exploits human beings. They continually have to tear themselves away from that economy by means of both the other two spheres of a healthy social organism if they are to avoid being exploited in and by the economy.

What tends to be called the social challenge doesn't persist in modern life in the same form as it arose, may potentially be addressed, and is then resolved. No, social challenges do exist, having entered life of late, and they will never disappear from human futures. As regards the future, there will be ever more social problems. Nor will they suddenly be solved by applying some measure or other, but they will instead find their resolution through people's continually and enduringly *willed* intentions, in which all that is used up in human terms by the economy will be offset by the legislative-rights sector from a purely political perspective, continually recompensing what has been exploited with spiritual content supplied by an independent spiritual-intellectual culture.

Those who have watched societal issues evolve over past decades—relatively speaking, it's not long since they reached their present proportions—those who have watched and inwardly accompanied the ways in which society has developed from its origins and the way in which social intentionality can be a decisive stimulus for the future structuring of human life, may have arrived at an idea which can be described as follows.

Many people—some quite enlightened among them—did not see society as having any social problems until a few decades ago. When I was young I became acquainted with an Austrian minister[30] who had a view of the Bohemian-German border and who came out with this ludicrous comment: 'Social problems stop at Bodenbach!' I well remember how the first social democrat miners marched past my parents' house on the way to their assemblies. I noticed then how social will emerges, not in the form of thinking about social movements but by experiencing them at first hand. I had to reflect that much would have to be undergone, that many mistakes would have to be made! Even many a socialist-leaning thinker of the time would make countless wrong assumptions. It would seem that people—especially in this area—are prone to developing their heads to the exclusion of their felt or lived experience. Mistakes of this sort extended horribly widely.

Out of a spirit arising from these observations, I have today tried to speak about social will, social intention. You, as members of a community of people looking ahead to what social willing can contribute to the recovery of humanity, invited me to address this topic.

Older people, such as I, have for decades been talking with people who often look back at all that had to be undergone over the course of arriving at today. Due to all that had to be borne, however, they come to the view that all those misfortunes were not completely in vain and that, even though the facts tell a sorry and often frightening story, people will be strong enough to find a way out of what is felt by a large proportion of humanity to be unsustainable, unbearable.

It is in this sense that I ask you to take on board what I have been permitted to say to you this evening; the facts themselves speak eloquently. They say quite clearly: The more vigorously those among you who are still young can honestly take up life-competent social willing, the more life-congruent will a smart and sound human society be.

***

Those who wish to ask questions are welcome to do so. Dr Boos, who gave a lecture a week ago, has declared himself willing to chair any discussion.

***

A member of the audience signals they wish to speak.
[Here there is a gap in stenographic notes.]

Dr Steiner replies: The point you raise takes its present form because you have overlooked what happens once you have given relative independence to the constitutional rule of law, on the one hand, and the economy on the other. Labour organizations, which will in part become associations of producers or consumer societies or indeed combinations of these, are only concerned with economic factors internally affecting the economy.

The governance of workers' rights falls within the remit of a relatively independent state, where nothing of an inter-personal nature, as I said, is determined outwith the democratic process. This is why I mentioned that, underlying such a purely democratic state—which forms a link between the other two spheres—is a layer where equality between individuals prevails under law. Here, the mere aspirations of each economic organization cease in the face of democratic rights because they are obliged to square those aspirations with the interests of other parties. So, that's what has to be done. The damage you describe will have to be remedied, damage which would definitely occur, for example, were working hours to be stipulated internally by economic powers themselves. Governance of the economy is restricted to that sphere alone, that is, to administering within the terms of workers' rights legislation. The setting of working hours is more the province of state bodies concerned with relations among individuals.

We should not forget the enormous changes that will take place between people once partisan interests are stripped away. Obviously, not everything will suddenly be perfect the world over; but unilateral interests will be eroded amid democratic state structures which have made equality among people their founding principle.

Just think: supposing, for example, a commercial organization has a vested interest, such as in a tight project deadline. It will have to put up with balancing that interest with those of others who would suffer under such a short timescale. If unconscious forces are ignored—rather like the parallel that natural organisms result in roughly similar numbers of males and females, obviously only approximately, which cannot be nor become a precise law of nature—then individual factors can work together in the social organism and nothing insufferable will result. Smaller individual interests will then be able to develop which would otherwise be in a broader sense damaging to others.

What underlies my way of thinking differs from that of many other modes of social thinking because the latter are more abstract. In terms of logic, you can easily distinguish one from the other, though a logical element may connect them. The vital factor here can always only be experience of real life.

Clearly, I cannot logically attest—neither can anyone—to whether in any social organism of the future no divergence of interests might occur. But you can assume that if forces are able to develop self-appropriately, then a humane evolution will follow. I mean, if you look at what I am suggesting—setting working hours to be removed from the economic process and into the sphere of state jurisdiction—then harm of the kind you mention will not arise in practice. That's what I'd say to that.

Another audience comment—stenographic record not available.

Rudolf Steiner: I might reply as follows to our respected enquirer. Clearly, every stand-alone lecture is disadvantaged to some extent in not being able to convey everything, and I don't know from which omissions in my lecture the respected enquirer has drawn the conclusion that I take no position on the psyche of modern workers, that I would take no account of recent workers' movements, and so forth. Everyone relates to this in their own way. For example, I was a tutor for many years, teaching many subjects at a workers' education institute and helped workers in trades unions and other political organizations with their training for speeches. I can therefore claim to be aware that large numbers of workers active in giving speeches in Germany owe something of their training to me. During that training, all manner of subjects were discussed including questions not in truth unconnected with the most inward, internal singularities of working-people's psyches or souls. I had no particular cause to highlight this aspect of my social involvement, so I don't know, but I cannot quite understand from which omissions from my lecture you take your assertion that I am supposed to be *in practice* totally remote from workers' movements.

Of course, it can be taken as read that within modern social movements it is working people themselves who are primarily to be considered. Just bear in mind how all evening I have been emphasizing how things look from a proletarian perspective. I have been talking about the proletariat as such. You will have noticed, had you listened closely, that it was precisely the point of my lecture to have set out in practical detail what I believe to be live issues among working people today.

As regards the objection that I portrayed too one-sidedly how I see the crucial basic fact of the bourgeois way of thinking being adopted by proletarian workers—that is, by their leaders—only highlighting it from isolated angles, my claim is supported by my detailed study of workers' outlooks, their perspectives and their entire movement.

I'd like to draw your attention to the following: a well-known Russian writer[31] whom I know personally, recently made me aware, in an odd context, how influential a philosophy espoused by younger people here in Zurich has become—that of Avenarius.[32] For its part, it has grown out of an essentially bourgeois bedrock. At least, I cannot imagine that Avenarius ever thought his philosophy would play the influential role among Russian workers' movements that it does today. As far as I'm aware, Adler[33] is very strongly represented here in Zurich, as also the science-derived philosophical persuasion of Mach.[34] Both these philosophical orientations are to some extent the official philosophy of Bolshevism,[35] of radical socialism. The Russian writer Berdyáyev says this in an essay—contained in a translation of the very interesting book *Russia's Political Soul.* Here Berdyáyev elaborates on that political soul most lucidly. I could give you numerous examples, many of which would be similar to those taken from the late Rosa Luxemburg,[36] and these would demonstrate to you that the last—and most mordantly significant for the workers' movement—legacy of bourgeois life and its mode of thinking is its scientific alignment. The ability to make spiritual life into an ideology is of bourgeois origin. The bourgeoisie, if one may use such categories, were the first to make scientific thinking tropes, knowledge of nature, into an ideology. Within their class they did not convert it into actual scientific thinking. That last ramification was left to proletarian thinking to conclude, albeit proletarian thinking had also drawn other conclusions. But it certainly drew on assumptions that are clearly recognizable as being firmly rooted in bourgeois scientific thought patterns. They just took them somewhat further. The significance of this should not be underestimated.

Those more deeply engaged in the whole matter and who have generated a deeper interest in the part the modern psyche plays in current workers' movements wait—on the one hand with some trepidation, I might say, but also with a degree of satisfaction, on the other—for the moment when all this will surface within the socialist movement. One day, what presently tarries at unconscious levels will be noticed and brought to consciousness. One day, this will be noted: Aha, we still retain this in our supra-psychic awareness—if I may call it that—in the upper reaches of our souls, and that has to come out. We have a longing to orientate our entire human dignity scientifically. The bourgeois scientific legacy has so far not made that possible. We need to look to a different spirituality.

I do, however, believe that the time will arrive when that reservoir of longing among what are possibly the only truly modern people, the proletariat, has surfaced. Though it has not yet come to full expression, this proletarian longing will have been expanded to its full iteration as a scientific method of thinking and become a philosophy of life possessing the power of the old religions. When that has set in, when working people are no longer considered commodities—because they will have woken up to that bourgeois implication—then the moment will have arrived about which you will be able to say that a productive structuring of social will has been achieved.

I do not believe you can relate quite so dogmatically to plain socialism, which the honourable enquirer has highlighted in the context of Bergson's[37] philosophy. I can obviously not go into philosophical details of that kind today. Our enquirer claims that Bergson is a typical representative of middle-class thinking. In that case the socialism originating in Bergson's philosophy will have extremely deep bourgeois roots! It can now be proved, for instance, that Bergson's philosophy is riddled with countless Schopenhauer-isms and that Bergson was vastly more influenced by Schopenhauer[38] than you can imagine.

Now, were you to explore an issue of this kind more comprehensively, you would indeed have to go into quite some detail. I cannot do that today, but I will mention that within the proletarian world there are those who are empathic thinkers, people such as Mehring.[39]

Franz Mehring, who is in many respects similar to Bergson, was the one to describe Schopenhauer as the epitome of philosophical petty bourgeois narrow-mindedness!

There can be many views on this and I don't believe you can be doctrinaire about them. You may take the view that Bergson is the most advanced philosopher while at the same time conceding that his philosophy contains irrational elements. But one wants to ask: What do irrational elements have to do with societal challenges? A proletarian worker can be just as irrational as a middle-class person. I really cannot understand what irrationality has to do with anything. You would have to make the following assumption: Bergson is the ultimate representative of modern philosophy; so if proletarians are to think correctly, they would need to be devotees of Bergson, wouldn't you say? That was the tenor of the entire question.

The tendencies of which I have been speaking have undoubtedly been occurring in the most varied fields of modern life. It would be deeply depressing were human existence to be continually, as it were, overdrawn—in the red, in deficit—to be heading in the opposite direction from that desirable as regards its evolution! This cannot happen, can it? For instance, I myself claimed that, among the judiciary, some quarters strongly inclined to psychologizing have been stoking matters. Countless such examples could be brought, but it would divert us off the main line into the sidings not to respond to the issue under discussion in favour of just airing pet opinions. Admittedly, one can sympathize warmly with some principles that today pertain more to what was said about stimuli active in past historical times, but without going into the latter in detail. To do so would delay us considerably. So, without going into them, I'd like to say: Many people remain mulish in attitude when there is any mention of threefolding, as I outlined today. You may well object that there cannot be three varying elements that are managed and led according to varying principles.

Yet I was not speaking of three differing spheres governed by three principles *at variance with* each other, but rather about threefolding the social organism! Just consider how this societal threefolding will eventually be found to be as compatible now with its entire thought structure as was the ancient configuration you find in Plato, which was appropriate to those times. Someone once said to me after a lecture: So here we go again, another reference to Plato's ancient stratification of society: producer-artisans, auxiliaries-fighters and guardian-philosophers! What I propose is the very opposite of this model divided into 'feed-fight-teach' because people are not divided into classes or ranks but rather an attempt is made at an organic societal whole. We human beings ought not to be compartmentalized! A person can perfectly well be as active in spiritual culture as in the judicial or industrial-economic spheres. This is precisely what liberates a person from exclusivity in any one area of the social organism. It is not a matter of people being divided into autonomous rankings when developing a healthy society but that the social organism is organized in harmony with its own inherent imperatives. That is the radical difference. Human societies used to be stratified. As appropriate to today's thinking, society needs to structure itself such that human beings can become active—each according to their circumstances, needs and capabilities—in relation to each sphere and to have an overview of the society in which each lives. For example, it will be quite possible for someone to be active in the economy while simultaneously holding office in the purely political state. In that case they would obviously have to pursue their economic interests differently from the way in which they would have done in the context of a legislative state. These three spheres will themselves take care of their territorial boundaries. There will be an end to the situation being so disordered and each sphere being entangled with the others.

Far better means will be found once there is a threefold division into areas. The faculties involved in differentiating will of course be the same. Yet, as is the case in the human organism—despite not wishing to create analogies—I would say that it contains three largely self-reliant elements: a nerve-sense system, a respiratory-lung-heart system and a metabolic system. Analogously, the healthy social organism will comprise three elements. This is something not yet embedded in our thinking habits, but which I do believe will eventually find its way into modern thinking and will, I hope, be accorded no less rigour than—in a manner of speaking—grappling with one's own pet opinions.

Dr Roman Boos: May I be permitted to respond to the previous enquirer with regard to what he asked about the sphere of criminal justice? If we are talking about a judge's freedom and whether an objection was also intended to the statement that no sentence could be handed down outwith legislature—but rather, as it seems to me, this was meant in the sense that criminal law should not itself issue from the spiritual-cultural sphere but that, from a political perspective, the question may contain a misunderstanding by Dr Weiss of the contention that it would be to breach the principle that nobody could be sentenced who had not contravened a specific law. Could I ask you kindly to comment on that?

Dr Steiner: This question is about the proximity of the public sphere of legislative rights with that of practical jurisdiction. What I was emphasizing was the *separation* of practical judging. That is why I used the term 'judging', expressly separating practical sentencing from general public rights legislation, which I had thought of as being beneficially centralized in the political state sector, so that the public rights in a healthy society would properly take responsibility for legislation being carried out in practice, which accords with laws as defined by itself. That verdicts cannot be handed down arbitrarily is obvious. But I hadn't thought about it like this, whose very abstractness makes it practically self-evident. Also, in exploring the social organism and social will, I haven't spoken about the effective reach of rights legislation. In the sense of our theme, I would ask you to consider the following.

You see, I have spent almost as much of my life in Austria as in Germany. I was able to become thoroughly familiar with Austrian life. Believe me, it is no impulsive assertion when I say that much of what has been going on of late in the so-called Austrian state is connected with events of the 1870s and 1880s and which caused deeply disjunctive disparities. Don't forget that in a nation such as Austria—I would not allow it to be described in such radical terms were it another nation, though this might exist in similar form elsewhere—where the three language areas have been thrown together haphazardly such that a German, if he happened to have a brush with the law in an area where a Czech judge unable to speak German presided, would be sentenced by a Czech judge in a language he could not understand, without understanding of what he was being accused and aware only that he was being hauled off. The converse would have been the case had a German judge sentenced a Czech unable to understand German. What I am talking about here is the free, one-to-one relationship between an accused individual and a judge.

So, a state such as Austria could have expected great things of a society structured as outlined above. A motivating impetus such as threefolding would have required five to ten years to implement—conditions shift continuously—at any rate, the accused or their accuser would have been able to choose their judge, at the free discretion of the judge.

[Here there is a gap in the stenographic record.]

This is not a matter for the sphere of spiritual culture but is from the outset one for *state* legislature. Because a verdict is dispensed on the basis of the single law in force at the time of a criminal act, the second societal area, that of state law as defined by its authoritative reach, will take care of the consequences, obviously according to its own criteria in each case.

However, the question is a different one. If you study things in greater detail you will see that the resolution of all such cases follow very, very consistently.

Today I was only able to describe very initial preconditions. Otherwise I would have to carry on talking not only all night but all day tomorrow as well.

Lecture 6

PUBLIC LECTURE, ZURICH, 8 MARCH 1919

What is the significance of blue-collar labour?

When today's lecture was announced, some may have wondered from which perspective the subject was to be tackled. Having asked around, you may have thought that this would be another of those areas of agreement so longed for by people who have been contributing to the current capitalist sea of social confusion, the ones who say that the water has already reached up to their necks but they are no longer in a position to swim in that sea. They look around for a lifeboat. They will search in vain for that lifeboat among the assumptions for which they habitually reach. It is no such perspective that is to inform this evening's talk. It seems to me that quite different things are required for the times in which we live. Let's look into what has actually been happening and what is being experienced by those so often in extremely dire circumstances who are searching for just such understanding.

What some call the social challenge arose by no means yesterday. In the way it is discussed nowadays, it is over half a century old. Yet what actually led to this social question is far, far older and includes all that prefigured developments over the last couple of centuries. When we look into what has resulted from those last centuries, we can summarize it briefly as follows.

There are numbers of people who might best be described as living off the capitalist economy and who feel pleasantly at home in that capitalist milieu. These can often be heard extolling the advances made by civilization. You would hear what could be achieved now that humanity was in a position to come to swift agreements not only between individual countries, but between continents right across the world and its oceans; and how far people had advanced to a point where a certain enlightened culture had become widespread, one in which people could participate in what they called culture or spiritual-intellectual culture, something imagined to have reached exceptionally high levels in our time.

Now, I don't need to describe the sort of fulsome praise of modern civilization being circulated. But this civilization has been spread via underground channels and would hardly be thinkable without these substrata, living as it did on the back of those very foundations. What exists in this submerged underworld? Ever increasing numbers of people have been living in this subterranean world, people of a kind who, from their most profound depths, have been bound to feel themselves chiming with the call: 'Give us what modern life has achieved, give us an existence worthy of humankind. To what has civilization condemned us?' In this way, contemporary humanity has increasingly been diverging into two constituent sectors: those who are largely feeling very comfortable—or at least quite contented—in modern civilization, but whose contentment is a result only of the fact that those in the other, suppressed, sector have been obliged to give their labour for a societal order in which they have basically been unable to have a stake.

Yet something else has been evolving as part of this whole course of events. It is that the leading figures of so-called civilization could no longer sustain the old patriarchal state together with its countless illiterate people. One development has been that those supported by capitalism at least had to educate the proletarians serving them in their employ. As a result of educating workers, something has come to expression, something those who understand history see as only too fearsomely inevitable. It transpires that these large numbers of people, who have had to provide the underlying foundations for modern civilization, had now been enabled to reflect on their own circumstances and were no longer obliged to be instinctively subservient but could ask the burning question: Are we living a life worthy of human beings? How can we achieve an existence worthy of being human?

Those who have hitherto been the leading echelons in society have, over the course of events—and to the extent that it benefitted them—brought economic life under the aegis of the state. And under these new conditions the proletariat can no longer be excluded from the state, not at least in any numbers. It was in this way that the proletariat were striving, on one hand, to transcend their position within the economy and, on the other, were aspiring for a humanly dignified life by trying to secure their rights with the help of the state.

It cannot be said—and present facts bear this out—that little has been achieved by both these means. Via trades unions, contemporary workers' associations have tried to make progress by various means within the circulating economy, but this has garnered just the crumbs of what really ought to constitute a dignified existence in a healthy economy. This has been accomplished via the state route; and solely by the stand taken against the economic and political power of society's hitherto ruling classes. So you can say that, despite a certain amount having been achieved via these two routes, modern working people remain no less challenged by the question: What value, what significance does my work have in relation to what each person the world over can claim in terms of their human dignity?

Faced with what had been called for by proletarians over the course of decades in the most varied forms, the riposte from these pre-eminent, leading circles has been: This cannot continue! In the face of this demand, barely a single understanding word has been forthcoming. Such words as were audible were curiously connected with what has been issuing from the spirit of the time and which ought to have constituted their aim. Have we not heard things being said from all possible quarters—from Christian socialists, from aspiring bourgeois-socialists—which could have averted the dangers they expected to see being unleashed? Aren't these, basically, just the soothing platitudes being issued by sundry traditional and upcoming religions, ethical-moral prejudices hailing from leading, once-pre-eminent classes?

Predominating echelons did not feel this. But another human stratum did feel it: those who were sensitive to things other than manners of speaking, who felt their course to be set by consciousness of their class, who were in the particular social situation of being the underlying foundations of modern civilization. Despite some progress having been made through trades unions, associative groupings and political routes, something else took shape, something more important, something representing the very labour of the contemporary proletariat, which is full of germinal potential for the future and which the present facts abundantly bear out. What took shape was that, while the hitherto leading classes were chasing luxury and wealth-creation—thanks purely to being nurtured and reinforced by capitalism—the proletariat, in the spare time allowed them, sought in their gatherings a modern education, schooling in the true sense of the word, and went in search of intellectual-spiritual culture. It was this that the hitherto pre-eminent echelons of society did not want to see: how across and throughout thousands upon thousands of proletarian minds and souls a totally new education and outlook on human existence was taking shape.

It was in the nature of things that this education initially took as its start the standpoint of observing economic life, because modern life had been forged by workers in industry, alongside machines. It had forced them into factories; it had harnessed them to capitalism. So it was here that they acquired their ideas. I only want to draw to your attention just how intensely and understandably did the impact of everything connected with Marxism strike home to proletarian minds. But these concepts and this educational offering was such that it found little—in truth barely any—resonance with those previously pre-eminent classes.

Isn't it typical that those in the know have to concede that, among leading proletarian personalities, among those who really understand working people and are not just given to cogitating *about* the proletariat, there are those who have actually absorbed what can usefully inform us about present economic life. Among them there really are those possessing a more thorough knowledge—that is, a thoroughness at least more grounded in real life—of what is at play in the social organism, knowledge more thorough even than that prevalent among the most educated of the educated, and this includes those pensive university professors of sociology. It is also typical of latter circles, where careers involve being conversant with sociology and political economy, that they repelled for as long as possible anything suggestive of empathizing with contemporary proletarians. Only when the facts crowded in, leaving them no other alternative, did a few of the leading bourgeoisie allow the odd Marxist or similar concept to be incorporated into their system of political economy.

It is not for drab theoretical reasons that I am claiming that the proletariat's labour was carried out for pre-eminent circles quite hidden from sight. I am saying this was the case because I could, with them, see to what their labour amounted. For many years I was a teacher at a Berlin workers' education college founded by Wilhelm Liebknecht senior. Partly at this college, partly at its affiliate, a good deal of the work being done to usher in a new era committed to advancing proletarian pan-human consciousness was taking place. By then, this should long have been appreciated by all those who were casually treating the proletarian movement as nothing more than a mundane wages-and-bread issue and who had no idea how to tackle it in terms of existential human dignity for all humankind.

On the other hand, it is not really surprising that today people allude to the resulting social chaos in the factual world and the awful, often harrowing, things happening there. Those who understand how matters have evolved do not query the context of this harrowing awfulness for the proletarian movement, but clearly take the view that it is those hitherto leading echelons or classes who are responsible for having brought about what is happening today.

It was a historically important moment when the proletariat started taking responsibility for events in that world history. Until and well into the terrible and fundamentally insane cataclysm of the so-called World War, capitalism and all that the capitalist system entailed have been responsible for subsequent—and particularly recent—circumstances.

What do we now see from the epicentre of all this in terms of the proletarian movement, proletarian longings, aspirations, demands and claims? From that pivotal point we see what working people had to experience when facing what they were in effect precipitating, the only thing that can now be provided by the economy to the social organism as a result of hitherto pre-eminent cultural circles basically showing no interest in working classes other than in this, their sole attribute: their labour. We need to realize just how incisive an impact the reflections of Karl Marx and those following in his tracks had on contemporary proletarians for the reason that they harboured a feeling, above all, that clarity had to be created regarding the ways and means by which human labour could be allowed to flow into the social organism.

Now, this has often been said and has been understood across wide swathes: as a result of the modern economic system, human labour has become a commodity among other commodities. It is a peculiar feature of the economy that it involves producing goods, circulating products and consuming that merchandise. Yet what has set in is that proletarians' labour has been commodified.

From an internal proletarian perspective everything has largely been said. Yet the question by which you acquire insight into the status of labour in a healthy social organism is largely side-stepped so that it never fully comes to light. A question therefore needs to be framed—albeit with a more precise and intense focus than follows from Marxist interrogation—thus: Can human labour ever be considered a commodity at all?

This is how the question is deflected onto quite different tracks. You will in fact ask: How can human labour be justifiably rewarded or recompensed? Is labour ever able to come into its own at all? And you could set the precondition that human work must indeed receive remuneration.

Remuneration, however, is in some contexts nothing other than the monetary purchasing power for the commodity called labour. Yet human labour can never be a commodity! Wherever labour is turned into a commodity in the economic process, that process is a deception, a falsehood, because something which can never be a true constituent of reality has been thrown into that reality. Human labour cannot be a commodity because the nature or quality necessarily innate in every commodity cannot inhabit labour. Within the economic process, every product must contain the potential to be compared with another product in terms of value. Comparability is a fundamental stipulation of a product *being* something. Human labour, on the other hand, can never be compared with any other commodity in terms of its inherent value.

It would actually be frightfully easy, had people only not *unlearnt* how to think. Just imagine, say, ten people in one family were to work together, each one doing their part, how you would calculate the contribution of one of these ten individuals with the combined output of all ten. You don't have the option of comparing the output of a product with that of labour. Labour is subject to completely different social grounds for appraisal from those of commodities. It is perhaps this that has not been expressed more explicitly of late but which nevertheless persists among the feelings of working classes.

What inhabits the demands of the proletariat? What is alive in their feelings is in fact *criticism*, is world-historic *critical censure*, which simply exists in the lives of proletarians and which is flung back at the demands imposed on them by previously leading circles by way of societal structures. The proletariat represents nothing other than harshly accusatory criticism on a global-historic scale. It is precisely the knowledge that labour can never be a commodity that owes its existence to the sensitivities, the underlying feeling, that in recent times a powerful and comprehensive *untruth* is being perpetrated, because labour is being bought, something it can never be according to its inherent nature.

It is clearly the belief of reasonable people and of workers themselves that a remedy has to be found. But these latter have been forced into a situation not of their own making but into what previously leading classes have made of society. Excluded from almost everything else, they are yoked into the economic process. Is it therefore not explicable that they want not only to restore the economic process to health—with its vital circulatory economic function—but also to contribute to the recovery of the entire social organism? This is where the ideals arose, in the configuration in which they have so far inhabited the proletariat.

It has been said that, due to capitalism—in the form of private capital from the private use of the means of production—modern production has been turned into a commodity industry and, as a result, the proletariat is said to have been driven into a situation which only they themselves can experience. They can only be helped by reaching backwards to the age-old idea of the *co-operative*, which is predicated upon each producing for the other, working towards self-production, in which nobody can cheat another because that would entail cheating themselves.

It has further been mooted how this great co-operative association might be created. You would have to take refuge in the framework which has been evolving over the course of recent times: in the state. You would have to turn the modern state into a huge co-operative, an association in which to some extent commodity production would be converted into production for one's own needs.

It is here that we must grasp the point about which it can be said: On the one hand, health is to be found specifically in the spiritual-intellectual culture of the contemporary proletariat while, simultaneously, finding in that spiritual culture what is capable of evolution and the point at which it can progress from the stage to which it has so far blazed a trail and from which it can once again progress to another level.

It should not be taken amiss by those of a differing opinion on this point that we are not yet seeing its ultimate success in the present proletarian outlook. This view is based on just as honest and genuine a perception as they too harbour. Yet one is obliged to point out that this proletarian outlook does contain within it the seeds for onward progression and that this progress requires real struggle. And that aim can be striven for.

Some admit to understanding what I was already identifying as an idiosyncrasy eighteen years ago, at the Berlin Trades Union Centre, and which I have since had cause to underline as being a singular feature of the modern workers' movement, something I still hold to be absolutely correct today. I said at the time: To those who can survey the historical evolution of human life and, from that perspective, can view the modern proletarian movement with understanding, having watched it making progress, it will have been conspicuous that this proletarian movement differs from all previous human movements ever to have existed in chiefly one respect, one which you may find bizarre or incongruous: it is constructed on scientifically-orientated foundations.

How deeply and intensely true is what the all but forgotten Lassalle[40] said in this regard about the underlying tone and challenge of workers' movements, which he touched upon in his famous speech about Science and the Worker. You just have to look at this from an angle differing from those prevalent today. You need to view it from the perspective of real life. You could say: from a perspective of what has become accessible to the proletariat. Or: what leading echelons have had to accord them if they wished to avoid relegating them to illiteracy. It was by these means that a proletarian gained the potential to inherit—much as in the manner of a legacy—what had accrued in modern times from the efforts of leading circles by way of a scientific world outlook.

The crux of the matter is that proletarians were to react differently to this scientific outlook from every other grouping, differently even from those who had created that outlook in the first place. Though you might be a highly enlightened person in hitherto pre-eminent circles, someone whose inner convictions spilled over from all that modern science had deduced, someone like Vogt,[41] for instance, or a popular natural-science researcher such as Büchner[42] you would relate differently to the scientific view than do proletarians.

Someone from leading echelons, with all their preconceived biases—or more precisely their *pre-felt sentiments* and selective vision—might theoretically commit to a modern form of studying humanity and nature but will none the less remain fixed within a societal order that is fiercely separated from the proletariat, a society whose structure and entire constitution does not originate in the narrative of modern science but rather from what once, before natural science, used to fulfil and stir human feelings through religious, righteous and similar ideas of human dignity. I was able to experience this at first hand in the following situation.

It was when I was standing alongside the recently so tragically departed Rosa Luxemburg in Spandau in front of a workers' assembly and we were both addressing them on the subject of workers and science. It was clear that what science could decant into proletarian souls has had a markedly different effect on proletarians from that which it has had on even the most staunchly dyed-in-the-wool among previously leading bourgeois echelons. As Rosa Luxemburg pointed out to assembled crowds: there is nothing to indicate human beings' angelic origin, nothing to indicate the lofty origins about which the bourgeois world view still likes to talk. Even the current bourgeois view still likes to claim that human beings descended from climbing animals and how they have upwardly evolved from that state. If you think that through—as that enthused workers' leader said at the time—you cannot persist in prejudices to which present leading circles subscribe, such as differentials in rank or status, nor should you opt to stratify humans, who all have identical origins, in the way those leading echelons do. This impacted workers quite differently from the way in which pre-eminent echelons would have received it, and it amplified what working people understood to be contemporary economic science.

Whatever is absorbed at a soul level is capable of onward development. It is about this onward development that I wish to tell you a little today.

Those having an overview across what is involved in the question: 'How has the labour of the present proletariat come to be seen as a commodity?' see themselves gradually being forced to take their observations about the economy to a point where they are obliged to reflect: it is because workers have been yoked solely into a life bound to the economy that within that economy proletarian labour has become a commodity. That line of thought leads only to a persistence of the slavery issue of old. At that time, the entire human being was a commodity. Now only their labour remains of that entire human being. And yet the whole human being is now obliged to follow in the footsteps of that labour.

Amid feelings in the proletarian psyche lies the potential for this to be prevented from applying in future, representing as it does a remnant of ancient barbarism still to be overcome. This will only be surmountable with the same clear spiritual force with which the proletariat has grasped both human nature and the economy, so that science can also be embraced in a healthy social order. I would like to say a few words about that science.

The following emerges clearly. We have to ask: What makes proletarian labour into a commodity within the circulation of that economy? It is the economic power of capitalism.

In the words 'the power of capitalism' lies a hint towards a wholesome answer. Because to what is power in diametric opposition? Power is positioned diametrically opposite the law and rights. However, that in turn implies that compensating for the devaluation of human labour within the social organism can only be brought about if labour—and the whole issue surrounding labour—is detached from, is lifted out of, the economic process as a whole and if it becomes purely and explicitly a question of law.

This leads us to consider the wider context and whether there is a deeper disparity between questions of the economy and those of law. Such variance does exist, though today one is not inclined to take it seriously enough. People are disinclined to take seriously enough the essential forces effective in all economic activity, on the one hand, nor, on the other, those necessarily affecting the sphere of legal rights.

What are the active constituents at work in the economy? Human needs are the catalyst for an economy together with the opportunity to fulfil those needs through production. Both are based on nature. Human needs are reliant on natural resources; production relies on climatic, geographic and related environmental factors. Under the influence of division of labour, the economy has led to a modern form of barter—which it is and which it ought to be—barter of the kind in which commodities are mutually valued or priced and, according to need or demand, come onto the market and are drawn into the circulating economy. I can't go into detail as it would take too long.

The sphere of legislative jurisdiction cannot at present also evolve as a self-contained rotation within the circulatory system of the economy. Human nature can as little admit that legal rights can develop, in the social organism and within the economy, as it will concede that the human body is controlled from a single centralized locus. I really don't intend to play around with natural-scientific comparisons tonight; I just believe that here is a point at which even natural science needs to transcend what it has become. In my last book, *Riddles of the Soul*, I alluded to a core issue insufficiently acknowledged by natural science: that the healthy human body contains three systems: a nerve-sense system, bearer of psychic-soul life, a respiratory-heart system supporting rhythmic processes, and a metabolic system supporting digestive activity, and that all three make the entire human organism viable. Each of these systems is self-centralized, each has its own ingress-egress with the external world. In the human body, order and harmony are generated not by these three systems interacting chaotically but by them developing alongside one another in such a way that the forces of each blend fittingly with those of the others.

A tripartite division or threefold structure ought to exist in a society pursuing optimum health. There needs to be an understanding that if a person is active in the economy, s/he is required only to do that specific job within the economic process. Then it is a matter for the governance or legislature of that economic process to proceed from a reciprocal valuation of the commodity in economic reality, mobilize it as appropriate into the circulation of goods, initiate commodity production and consumption. In this basic economic model we need to exclude whatever relates to the fulfilment of need between single individuals in favour of the relationship between every individual and *every other* individual. The capacity in which everyone has to be equal differs radically from what can potentially develop within the economy alone. That is why it is essential for the recovery of the social organism that the legislative sphere, that of rights per se, be removed from purely commercial activity, something which in recent times has been strenuously opposed.

What have those previously leading classes done? In areas convenient to them—areas which seemed to coincide with their own interests—they further promoted that old amalgam, which had existed so widely, between economy and state-politics. That is why we see—precisely under the aegis of those pre-eminent circles—increased nationalization or state control of certain branches of industry. Nationalizing postal, telecommunications and other such bodies was considered reformist and fundamental to their desired progress.

Those not focusing on the interests of hitherto leading circles need to think along diametrically opposite lines. They should be asking: What are the foundations underlying a healthy social organism? They should be aiming for purely economic activity to be increasingly detached from state activity as such, and for the state area responsible for law and order to be responsible above all for ensuring that appropriate legal rights flow from its sphere of influence *into* the economy. In life, those lacking the eyes, the spiritual eyes, to discriminate properly fail to see how radically different are economy and political states as such.

Let's look at the way in which things have developed. Some people say of the present social situation that, firstly, we have the exchange of goods for goods. Fine, that is a given in the economy and we have already touched upon it. Secondly, they say—and feel justified in so doing—there is the exchange of goods and by extension the exchange of a representation of goods i.e. money for labour. And thirdly: an exchange of goods for legal rights.

What is this last item? I have discussed the second. Now we just need to look at property ownership in a modern economy. What needs clarifying for the future in this respect will then become instantly clear to us. Whatever one may usually think about ownership of land—everything else has little significance for real societal processes—the only aspect of any substance is that landowners have sole right of use of a parcel of land and may thereby assert and further their personal interests.

As far as its origins are concerned, this has nothing whatsoever to do with the economic process. Only a perverse political economy could object to the following statement. *Only* what is produced on land by way of products—or has the value of a commodity—has anything to do with the economy. Use of land relies upon a legal right.

Within the present capitalist economic system—and specifically due to the amalgamation of capitalism with ground rents—this right mutates into a form of coercion. This is how we have, on the one hand, power or coercive governance, as an exclusion from those rights; and on the other, such economic power as can coerce human labour into becoming a commodity.

From both these sides, nothing less than a real-life deception is being perpetrated where there is no aspiration—no genuine striving based on social insight—to structure society into an economic sphere and politics-and-state in its limited definition.

The economic element will have to be established on an *associative* basis, informed by the needs of consumers and their relationship with producers. Based on the various interests of a wide range of professional groups, a great variety of associations or co-operatives—you could also call them by their old name of brotherhoods—will have to be cultivated in which the predominant ethos will be one of *need-fulfilment.*

Whatever develops from this associative basis of the economy will always be concerned with one group of people fulfilling the needs of another such group. The decisive factor in this respect will have to be, firstly, competent pricing of natural resources and, secondly, expert design of the means of producing the goods, the logistics of their circulation and their consumer base. Here too, the decisive factors are human need and human interest.

This will always be considered something radically different from the framework in which every person is seen as basically the same as every other person, in that they have to be considered equal, as in the often trivialized words: Everyone is equal before the law etc. which implies the same in face of a law they have themselves created as equal human beings.

The circulatory process of the economy will have to be based on associative foundations. The body politic, as a restricted entity, will be constructed on purely democratic bases, incorporating the principle of equality *of* all people and *in relations between* all people. Something quite distinct will ensue from this body politic, something different from the economic *power* that makes human labour into a commodity. From this political body, once separated from the economy, genuine workers' rights will evolve, in which labour is to be handled in *solely*—purely—human, inter-personal terms. Here, too, labour rates and conditions will be negotiated and agreed.

Though you may believe that matters have improved in recent times, basic underlying principles have not advanced. Due to the way in which proletarian labour is treated throughout the economy, the price of labour-become-commodity will be dependent on the value of other commodities within that industrial economy. Anyone looking more deeply into the economic process will be able to appreciate that. Things will look different once purely democratic employment legislation and governance is instated—independently of the economy and its governance—and is instead delivered by the political-state. What will then transpire?

What will then happen is that whatever a person is able to contribute to the social organism by dint of their labour will exist in as dynamic and self-determined a correlation as today applies to natural resources. Technically, and within certain limits, the fertility of soil, of land and so forth, can be slightly modified and nature's hard and fast capacities somewhat upgraded. Yet, from one perspective, it is these natural resources that overwhelmingly dictate the economy. Just as in this respect the economy is externally demarcated, from another perspective the economy also has to be externally restricted in the form of no longer making labour dependent on it, such that labour—out of purely *human* causal imperatives—can be offered to the economy. Then labour dictates the price of commodities and the commodity no longer dictates the cost of labour!

At worst, what might then happen if for some reason the workforce were not able to deliver satisfactorily, economic activity would be depleted. This could be remedied by seeking help from legislative-judicial sources and not merely from within the economy.

Solely underlying the economy is the principle of supply and demand. With employment law on the same footing as that of an independent state-political entity, it will be necessary to place all other rights on that same footing. In short—and I can only hint at this due to time constraints—it will be essential for the ideal of a healthy future society to see that these two spheres are peeled apart: legislature-and-rights from industrial-economic activity.

And, thirdly, the now-independent economy and judicial systems will be joined by what we can call a culture of intellectual-spiritual human activity.

It is especially when speaking about this genuine progression of a proletarian world view that you will on the whole encounter opposition, because on this issue the opinion has been subsumed into habitual thought—possibly more so here than in other areas—that only by absorbing cultural-spiritual activity wholesale into the state can the latter bring about humanity's salvation. People cannot yet grasp the state of dependence into which intellectual culture has of late become ensnared by the state, and how this has come about as a result of their interests, that is, the interests of those of pre-eminent echelons being so gratifyingly served by that state. These formerly leading circles have seen their interests well served and have allowed what they know to be cultural activity to be increasingly sucked into state functions. Just as the state is obliged to levy taxes, bring about equality of all people before the law and, through compulsory tax legislation, to meet their needs so, equally, must culture be thoroughly liberated from the other two elements of the social organism.

It is precisely what has of late been pursued in this respect—the amalgamation of cultural-spiritual activity with state- and economic spheres—that has caused such calamitous damage. Because what belongs amid cultural activity can only evolve in the light of true freedom. Anything not given that light to develop fully and freely stultifies and paralyses genuine spiritual culture, leading it awry, as we unfortunately see only too often in the present social order. What is needed in this spiritual sphere is to see through to what sort of inner connection exists between closely defined spiritual and religious activity, with scientific activity, artistic endeavour, life in moral-ethical terms: what the connection is between all this activity and everything arising from individual human abilities and the array of dextrous craft skills.

Because serious issues for healthful social living are being discussed in earnest here, we are including in spiritual-intellectual culture everything to do with advancing culturally, unfolding and cultivating individual capacities, everything to do with schools from nursery to university, right into art and ethics, yes, even into those branches of culture which provide a basis for practical and economic life. In all these areas, the aim must be to emancipate culture, so that this cultural element can be located within the free initiative of individuals who have relevant capabilities. That is free cultural living, which can only flourish in a healthy society if it comes fully into its own, freely garnering the recognition and understanding of those by whom it needs to be received. This means that cultural life can no longer be somehow left out of calculations involving sums of monetary wherewithal available in pocket and coffer, nor can culture be governed by state bureaucracy.

It is not only due to being governed by the political state that spiritual culture has assumed a certain quality reflective of the personalities involved in its administration, but spiritual-intellectual culture, in the form we now have it—which is understandably perceived by proletarians as an ideology—has also become a reflection of the interests and needs of dominant classes for and through the state, formed in the image of their own leisure and comfort, suiting their own requirements. Is it ultimately acceptable for spiritual culture to merely be a reflection of, or an adjunct to, the economy and the political state? The culture of leading echelons is just such an adjunct or addendum. Admittedly, it is not in the nature of chemistry and mathematics to take on characteristics issuing from the interests of leading circles. Not the extent alone in which they are performed, but the light in which they are viewed by other branches of culture, is determined by the interests of dominant circles—those hitherto leading echelons—where the interests of the state are being merged with culture within that state.

It is particularly in these most important fields that spiritual culture should be taking beneficial hold of hearts and minds and establishing its place within social life that culture has become the plaything of the economy and the political state. Right into these catastrophic times of war, we can see in the way in which leading lights in culture are bound via capitalist detours to the state, causing this most vital spiritual constituent of society to generate what should by rights be placed in the service of a modern nation.

Proof of this can be found not a hundredfold, not a thousand- but many a thousandfold. You just need to consider one thing: take German history professors, custodians of historical sciences. Try to picture everything they have produced on the history of the Hohenzollerns and ask yourself whether, after recent world events, Hohenzollern history will look just as it did beforehand. Then you will see how, through circumstances, spiritual culture has just become a mirror image of everything from which it has failed to free itself.

Spiritual-intellectual culture has to break free of the other two societal spheres. Then culture will be able to bring under its own aegis and within its own intrinsic lawfulness whatever ensues from capitalist prejudice. Then, however eccentric or startling it may sound to some, spiritual culture will really be capable of transcending purely economic proletarian interests. For spiritual-intellectual culture is a single totality. Spirituality cascades from the loftiest regions right down into all those branches of culture which arise due to someone—thanks to their individual capacities—taking the lead in some enterprise or activity. In the way culture has been directed to date, it proceeds from the economy, under the forceful imperative of economic coercion. How it ought to be conducted in a healthy social organism is out of spirituality itself, which has its own legislature and governance at the highest levels, but which will also comprise all spirituality working into economic processes—that is, once spiritual culture has secured its independence.

Then the influence of a liberated, independent cultural sphere will be properly experienced among economic processes. Then it will no longer be possible for everything accomplished through capital to have been achieved within parameters of present capitalism, but what it does fulfil will be at the behest of purely spiritual incentives.

Now, you have to imagine these motivating forces correctly. What would an industry under such stimulus actually look like?

Those who are familiar with cultural-spiritual initiatives down into their very foundations know—as I do very well—and will not contradict me when I give the following description of a business which takes its motivation not from economic dominance but from spiritually-inspired power. Because of the unencumbered understanding they share with their co-working colleagues, they will be in a position—by drawing on certain capital funding—to undertake trade not for their own benefit but conditioned by a social understanding they will have garnered from relevant spiritual sources. A business of this kind will contain someone occupying a leading role, with the free agreement of their colleagues at all levels, and, because this collegial agreement exists between business leader and employees, it will necessarily follow that—within each business and within associations of businesses—there will be opportunities outside working hours for free debate as to the way in which that particular business operates within the overall economic and social organism. Within the ambit of a spiritual-cultural influence such as this, the person then tasked with replacing what is at present the role of a capitalist entrepreneur will be responsible for the implications their product will have for human society as a whole.

Then each individual will understand the path taken by the product to which their labour has contributed, from those crafting products by hand to those who, on account of their specialized individual capabilities, are directing their manufacture. This alone will give workers the option to enter into genuine employment contracts; because these cannot exist under conditions that view labour as a commodity. Proper employment contracts cannot allow of any such premise, but can only be framed around agreement that the labour required to produce a given product be carried out with appropriate legislative backing. But further that, in terms of the economy, co-operative, collective involvement be instated among both manual blue-collar and intellectual white-collar workers, such that this necessary allocation of labour between manual and intellectual roles proceeds from a free understanding that manual workers know—because of the spiritual-cultural understanding they share with management—to what extent their work accrues to their own benefit within the social organism.

It is only under such collaborative conditions that enterprises necessarily based on capital will cease being able to operate for personal, egotistical advantage. It is only then that the social organism will be healed and today's profit incentive be replaced with purely objective, factual interest. Then, also, will the connection between an individual and their work, such as existed more widely in times gone by, be revived.

Let's look at today's connection with work. On the one hand you have entrepreneurs who carry out what they see as work but from which they remove themselves as swiftly as possible. Once they have made themselves scarce from work, they dismiss all talk about work as shop-talk. They make their escape and—by all sorts of diversionary means—seek to pursue their own personal goals. This sort of relationship with work illustrates how little people identify with their work.

However, this is a toxic attitude which has consequences for others, in that the proletariat of today has been torn from its traditional grounding in the crafts, where they felt a bond connecting them with their trade, deriving their sense of honour and human dignity from it, to now being harnessed to machinery, installed in factories, where that unsalutary attitude is generated that prevents individuals from identifying with their work.

However, those who recognize the true scope of spiritual potential will know that such noxious relationships between human beings and their work can only arise out of equally harmful preconditions. There is nothing in wholesome spiritual-culture—when it is free of politics, free of economics, yet *affecting* both these—there is nothing within such intellectual culture that is not immediately interesting and which—when rightly handled—cannot connect people with their work, if they know that their work will become an element in all that circulates throughout the societal organism. The fact that people also have to engage in uninteresting activities should not be deemed something that cannot be otherwise. No, the foundations of spiritual culture should be considered something to be sought after, something which alone can stimulate interest in—and connection with—every domain, including that of each person with their working context.

It will transpire that, once a freely liberated spiritual culture is able—from sources of spiritual influx—to inspire all the various branches of state and economic life, right down to supporting their custodian-administrators, that only then will truly objective interest be kindled in everything instead of solely in ratios of external trading advantage.

Certainly, the foundations for spiritual culture of this kind have to be created. Such foundations can only be elaborated once all education is placed under the tutelage and protection of a spiritual-intellectual sphere and when the lowliest teachers no longer have to wonder what the political state requires of them, but when they can look up to those they trust, to those who can administer the cultural-academic sphere according to their own lights.

This is largely how the effects of what I believe to be in tune with natural lawfulness ought to arise. This is really a genuine extension of a proletarian world view which can work to counter habitual thinking. For whilst bourgeois science left a legacy of having intermixed spiritual-culture, state and economy, it is for the purpose of reviving society that the aim should be to make the three spheres we are discussing independent of each other. Only if these three domains have—if I may use an approximation—their own 'parliaments' or governing bodies, each relating to the others as between governments of sovereign states, negotiating only through delegation, exchanging only matters of common need or concern; only then will society be returned to health. The question today is the fundamental challenge behind all the facts: How can society be restored to health? This has to be taken in hand. The social organism is ailing!

To those who, on the basis of their class consciousness, are to mount a justifiable claim to restore the social organism: you need, initially, to pursue the proletarian world outlook to its germinal source and from there develop it appropriately.

I expect some initial exception to be taken, on the grounds of what some consider to be acceptable, when I reiterate that social threefolding is the course of action that needs to be taken, a tripartite social organism. However much this may go against the grain of their habitual thinking, reality cannot be expected to adapt just for our convenience, nor to placate those who have always claimed to be practical people, astute and savvy in everyday life. Reality has to be congruent with what is honest and based on a robust sense of truth capable of recognizing what is right.

What I have been explaining doesn't apply to some cloud cuckoo land. Oh, the times are not far off when a few people—because they can only handle the simplicity shaping their thought patterns while deeming themselves practical people—will have to admit that those frowned-upon, fiercely scorned idealists who think in terms of humanity's evolutionary needs turn out to be the truly practical ones. What I have outlined is no cloud-cuckoo fantasy but is derived from humanity's most immediate everyday living needs.

I cannot of course go into every single aspect. In conclusion I want to touch on just one issue, in which I will show, albeit only in passing, how the prime thinking on social living I have been positing addresses the direst of problems. What is one of the grittiest areas in life? A thorny issue is that we are obliged to carry around what we call money. But you know what money entails and how it intrudes in all life. When focusing on the development of a wholesome social organism, under the auspices of which sphere does administering or managing money belong?

Governance of money has, due to certain longstanding evolutionary dynamics, been the remit of the state. Yet in a healthy society money is just as correctly a commodity as labour is no such commodity. Everything about money that affects the social organism toxically is embodied in the fact that today money is largely stripped of its commodity quality by being embossed with some emblem by the political state rather than—because international trade can proceed in no other way—relying on what it ought to represent: its value as a commodity. Political economists wage an amusing fight, an argument that strikes the wise as droll. They query whether money is a commodity—albeit a favourite commodity—which can always be swapped for other commodities. Whereas otherwise if you, for instance, had the misfortune to manufacture only tables and chairs, you would have to drag them around with you, waiting for someone who might swap vegetables for furniture; or you could exchange tables and chairs for money to their value beforehand, paying money for such goods as you immediately need. Whereas some claim that money is a commodity—or at least the representative of goods, even if it may be in the form of notes—for which a corresponding value in goods must exist, others claim that money comes about largely because the state legislates for certain emblems to be embossed on coinage. So now political-economy boffins investigate: What is correct? Is money a commodity? Or is it something that only occurs because it is minted? Is it just a token of a commodity?

The answer to these questions is simply this: money is neither one thing nor the other, but is both. It is the one thing because the state mints a particular currency; it is the other because in international trade or in certain circumstances within national trade, money is purely a commodity which can circulate among the general circulation of other commodities.

A healthy social organism will divest money of its legalistic attributes. Via its own normal processes it should be assigned—including depositing money, minting money, determining the value of money within the circulation of the economy—to the same parliamentary-type governance and legislative framework as operates the rest of the economy.

Only when this is introduced can the goal towards which the proletariat should be aiming be established on a sound footing. As regards that peculiar correlation which exists between wages and their commodified nature, this relationship is actually built on a life-sized falsehood. Whilst on the one hand workers believe—by demanding higher wages—that when this has been achieved to their satisfaction they will have gained ever healthier conditions, on the other hand the price of goods will continue to rise unless economic circulation is freed from the legislative flow of the political state. All this will only have been put on a sound footing once threefolding has been introduced.

Similarly, if you understand the spiritual independence essential to culture, you will also grasp that there is no prerequisite to create capitalist businesses as such. Instead, the ways and means by which capital has been governed in recent times and how it has been used—due in turn to the fact that it alone exists in the economic process—this is how capital, through its effects, has caused such parlous damage and much associated misery.

It will have to be understood that as long as employment contracts fail to apply to the common element shared by what both manual and intellectual worker together produce, and as long as employment contracts refer to payment for work, it will be impossible to put them on a sound footing.

Solely by granting to spiritual culture its salutogenic reality will it be confirmed that in every case where workers are exploited—in that vital relationship between workers and their intellectual management—that they are not only duped by the economy but fleeced by entrepreneurs who improperly devalue their personal-intellectual qualities in a way that is also counter to the law and which degrades human dignity. Workers are not just exploited by the economy but by that life-sized deception that arises from a societal organism where individual qualities can be used to take advantage of workers. Because within the economic process this is not bilaterally visible; whereas within a salutogenic intellectual sphere this will be transparently observable from both perspectives and controlled accordingly.

As I said, I can well understand if what I am introducing for societal healing may still antagonize some proletarian souls. I understand that; because for years I have been discussing this with working people. Not only was I in charge of education in several subject areas but I also coached workers in speaking, during the course of which all sorts of issues were raised among this working community that illustrated the specific nature and complexion of their demands. Here you learn to consider proletarians not just in the way present—or indeed previous—leading echelons do or did. No, you learn to think *with* workers not just *about* them.

It is my intended stance—and I want you to understand this—that though perspectives on the content of opinions may vary here or there, that at this present moment in world history it is not a matter of whether you disagree with this opinion or the other, but that you find consensus by empathizing with the honest demands that are necessarily those of contemporary proletarians. It is purely in coming in empathic terms to such a consensus, to a consensus forged in honest will, it is solely in this accord that the germinal seeds of their onward evolution can be found in proletarian world views. Because the time for just discussing is over; the time is over when those only wishing to serve their own interests can be allowed to speak of understandings and agreements. The time has come for the proletarian undercurrents and demands of decades' standing to emerge onto the platform of world history, there to feature among the most significant, the most pressing phenomena in modern times.

What has emerged from the chaos of economic strife and wide-scale war, what has prevailed for a long time and may persist in exaggerated form into the future will become *the* socially challenging question. It has not been my intention to present anything unrealistic, some theoretical panacea nor anything of that ilk. I wanted to make you aware that the time has dawned when, for the sake of people's collective, co-operative living, society ought to be structured into separate constituent components: of state, economy and cultural-spiritual domains, and that, as a result of this salutary and salutogenic restructuring, a sustainable and enduring solution to the social challenge is able to proceed.

This social challenge will not be resolved from one day to the next once it has been raised. But because the issue will be ever-present—much in the way that life incessantly creates new conflicts—threefolding will always be necessary to structure human society as it struggles to resolve, in all honesty, the conflicts arising in society. Whether any attempt will be made across the world to grasp that it is upon the progressive evolution of a proletarian world view that future social healing rests will depend on which direction is taken by a modern proletarian movement from that point forwards. All the justified challenges and demands surrounding wages-and-bread require that progress really has to escalate into becoming a vast, world-historic transformation which will progress from present proletarian consciousness, advancing to become universal human consciousness. What others have hitherto been unable to establish will then, founded in the dignity of contemporary proletarians, be established as true human dignity for all humankind.

***

In the subsequent discussion, several members of the audience expressed their views. The following formed Rudolf Steiner's closing words.

Rudolf Steiner: Yes, to begin with, in response to our first honoured speaker, I must make something of a general remark. Very often, when speaking, one is obliged to say that one doesn't fully understand why things in the form expressed by our first speaker have to be said exactly as though they were refuting what one had oneself just said. The first speaker spoke as though he felt compelled to oppose me in every last detail—while acknowledging some aspects at least in terms of general stance. I am not in a position to have to retaliate, but have to say that in fact I think that those who listened to me properly won't have much against what the first speaker said. As regards content, I am able to acknowledge even more than what he seemed to be focusing on in terms of expressing what I intended.

Now, one detail seems important to me. It is remarkable that our first questioner believed it necessary to emphasize that what I said was a result of talking with workers rather than working with them. Clearly, each person can only be effective in their area of competence. But the way in which I worked with those workers was such that it cannot be said that we merely talked among ourselves. I also believe that those possibly more attuned to the whole impetus of today's lecture will appreciate, in terms of its overall intended *will*, that I have not been spoken to in this way for years, though I am aware that today I am being thus addressed. I haven't been spoken to in this way for years, if only for the simple reason that in those days the workers already felt that what I had to say was not said just for the sake of chatting.

Honestly, that it has become possible for me to speak in the way that I had to today is no hastily acquired skill. Let's raise the question: Who can actually count themselves among proletarians? Someone who—through force of destiny and their own efforts—has come to be accepted by speaking with and to workers as I could in my capacity as an independent lecturer. Because in the communal circles, in which I am accused of participating, I have been treated as badly as—if not worse than—today's treatment. It is something different if one has worked as relatively hard as I have, something I will continue for my few remaining years. For years I earned acceptance by conversing, working and going hungry with workers[43]. I didn't 'ask postal worker what it took to go hungry'. I myself had to go hungry with them. Because the family in which I grew up was probably in far more dire straits than all the 'postal workers' whom one might question today. I didn't only come to understand proletarians by learning to think about them. No, I came to understand them by *living with them*, by myself growing up in working-class conditions, finding out about and experiencing hunger first-hand. From a background such as this—working for years on end among other working people—it could even then be felt that I was in a position to speak, not theoretically, but on the basis of thoroughly relevant experience. I think that provides a valid basis as to whether or not one has the right to speak with proletarians.

That is what I wanted to say in response to the one matter.

A large part of what the first speaker said did not refer to me but to intellectuals in general. Yes, our chairman has already said: If anyone can talk of having had mud thrown at them, that is, mud thrown by intellectuals, then I can do so, too. In fact, were you to follow up the ways in which mud—in its many varieties—has been thrown in my direction, you would probably not envy me my dealings with intellectuals.

This is a personal remark among what are altogether personal remarks. But the ripostes received are also basically of a personal nature, which is why such remarks as were made had to be made.

Now, much was obviously not referring to me but to the student body. As regards this latter: do you think I don't entirely concede that a majority of today's students feel justifiably criticized that their ideals don't stretch to the lowest-paid workers? Much could obviously be said about this chapter, but it is precisely today's workers, on the other hand, who ought to understand that—just as other classes or echelons have developed among people—students are ultimately also a product of their circumstances. Those who can compare the striving within today's student body even-handedly with what, for instance, was encountered among students when I was a student—it's a long time ago now—would say that albeit in respect of the thorough decline of the bourgeoisie in which current professors are entangled—on which students are obviously obliged to be reliant—with regard to the example that lit the way for today's students, one can, after all and for everyone's sake, entertain a certain satisfaction in the way students flourish in pursuit of improvement. Even though it may appear as though the student body were stabbing workers in the back, collaborators will emerge from the student body, possibly in large numbers, who champion social ideals. Students have quite a lot to overcome. Let's not forget how tight the shackles are that restrain us all. I have recently had many opportunities to talk with students about things which may seem remote in terms of their immediate ideals, but which are close to what can in general be termed mental health and spirituality, such as must evolve out of today's spiritual malaise. I know what receptivity there is among young people for a renewal of spiritual life. I also know how great the temptation is, once the enthusiasm of youth is behind you, for those who have graduated and need to find a job in present bourgeois society, just how great the temptation is to sink into petty bourgeois narrow-mindedness.

We won't arrive at any ultimate resolution to all that we hope and long to see from one day to the next. But we ought to accept that, wherever longing and understandable desire for what the proletariat rightly demand gains ground, it should not be suppressed by dogmatically or zealously conflating one with the other. Yet I do believe that any such dogmatism must be mollified, at least to some degree, even if the means in the present struggle cannot be too loosely chosen, when faced with the attitude I spoke about in my lecture: that it ought to be less a matter of thought variance than *equality of honest will.*

So, just ask yourselves how many of those you claim would stab you in the back are dependent on the circumstances in which students find themselves while, on the other hand, also asking yourselves how much *honest will* is being exerted among today's young people. Nurture that honest will rather than reverting to dogma that in practice incapacitates you.

Now, as to what the second speaker put forward, I can say this in reply: I agree with the call which came from over there on the left, that it is basically not so very different from what I myself said. I am not set on things being said exactly as I said them. Let's just say, if something contributes to improvements, I am delighted. Because of this I don't want to judge too harshly what the second speaker said differently. I just want to clarify something which suggests that the second speaker has not quite understood accurately. He is suspicious of my claim to have taught for many years in a college for workers in Berlin to the extent that he says he supposes it will only have been some liberal workers' association. I said clearly that it was the Workers' Education College founded by the senior Wilhelm Liebknecht. I don't believe you can credit Liebknecht senior with having founded such a multiplicity of workers' colleges that the workforce of those days would not gladly have accepted them. Listeners were not 'drawn from among the usual bourgeois liberals' but only working people from proletarian backgrounds and social democrats, as organized by the bank!

That's why I think some of my words may have been misunderstood by our gentleman speaker, taken to be other than intended, other than can be grasped if from the outset preconceptions are not brought to bear on the differing views of others—let alone when one agrees with what they are saying, albeit in slightly different form. And because they believe it necessary in this world-historic moment for things to be taken more comprehensively, believing that not everyone who makes snap judgements can be called practical nowadays whereas truly practical people have an overview of the broader picture.

As for the idea of an appeal or petition, which was mentioned: this is almost literally identical with what I was saying to you this evening. So, having heard that I myself formulated that appeal or petition, you won't be surprised nor will you expect me to speak differently when addressing bourgeois audiences from the way in which I have been speaking to you from this lectern.

Objection: Either it is the same everywhere, or…

That is just what I said. I reiterate: the same is written in the appeal as I have been saying here. Nowhere in that appeal is there anything other than what I have said here.

To me, the salient thing is that what I say is, in its very essence, the truth. I will speak the truth in whichever locality I am permitted to do so. Speaking the truth is what counts for me; the truth is what I have to convey. I will never exclude anyone from anything if they can square it with their convictions and say yes to what I have to say. Because I believe that it is only by speaking the truth—unencumbered by the impression it may make on people, whether signed, in print or not—that we can make progress towards *green shoots.* That's what I want to say about truth.

Then, in conclusion, I would like to make one remark in response to what the next questioner said: that I had said nothing about the manner of the struggle. Implied throughout my words the sense could be intuited as to what I actually think about the means of struggle. I think I indicated fairly clearly that in my view it cannot be a matter of arriving at some superficial appraisal, or whatever they call those nice neat outcomes. Today we have moved into a factual phase, where the only option is to actually *avoid* arriving at aimless opinions as to how things ought to be changed, and instead aspire to an outlook that really enables new ideas to take hold of human hearts. Because old thinking has shown what kind of social order it produces. Old thinking provides its own proof that it is past all usefulness. That is why I believe that for immediate, instantly practical reasons, it is above all a matter of those who have *honest social will* coming to agreements about what can be done in given situations.

Today we are in Switzerland—I'm not sure whether to say 'thank God' or 'unfortunately'—and still in circumstances that differ from those in Central and Eastern Europe. These latter remain embroiled in circumstances which can only be handled constructively by linking with this fundamental, archetypal thinking to inspire society. If, initially among the proletariat itself, attempts are not made to discuss such fundamental issues and, out of the present chaos, to start implementing these ideas throughout the least complex organizations—all of which must, in my opinion, be socially threefolded—if among the proletariat itself healing is not brought about, with new thinking inspiring the founding of new enterprises, I see no immediate salvation occurring over the coming decades.

Above all, we will have to begin from what may be considered a marginal standpoint. We need to understand that we are not only faced with bourgeois infrastructure and bourgeois environmental conditions but bourgeois science to boot.

That is what I was saying in the Berlin trades unions sixteen years ago and which was correctly understood by proletarian members themselves. Workers still have the prime task of purging their thinking of bourgeois science, not setting up societal facilities in any way aligned with bourgeois science but, instead, being inspired by this new thinking, thinking which is possibly only intelligible to proletarians because they are unshackled from other social contexts unfortunately inhabited by bourgeois people.

Though it may seem the least significant sphere to you, it is why what most urgently needs to be actioned today is to emancipate spiritual-intellectual-academic culture, to create freedom in spirituality. Healing will only be effected if we get to the point of thoroughly ensuring a free spiritual culture, if we can guarantee that science—once it no longer owes allegiance to capitalism, is no longer in hock to capitalism—can set the tone right into proletarian circles. I do not seek a narrowing but a widening of proletarian responsibilities.

However much people object from a standpoint similar to that of our second questioner—which I can well understand—arose by failing to grasp sentence for sentence what I was saying. I am firmly of the belief, gleaned over a long life spent among the proletariat, that what I have been saying will initially not be understood by other classes but precisely by working people themselves. It is unfortunately likely to take quite some time before it is widely understood, yet I am certain that *there* it can be taken up.

With these thoughts I would like to say that I can look back to what I had hoped to achieve today with a certain satisfaction. I honestly did not set out to convince you in every last detail or word. I respect the freedom of your personalities—the freely generated comprehension of all those present—too much to have done so. I believe that among you many may now think differently about what I have been saying from the way in which you were thinking earlier today. And it is from this belief that I draw the inference that this thinking is integral to healing the social organism.

RUDOLF STEINER'S NOTES FOR THE SOCIAL CHALLENGE

ABOUT *these notes:* With the exception of material for Lecture 4 of 12 February 1919, written notes (*Notizbucheintragungen* Nb 97 and 130) referencing these lectures are not dated by Rudolf Steiner himself. This is probably attributable to the fact that they form the conceptual framework for a series of lectures on the same topic planned within a short timescale in several localities, of which only those held in Zurich are published in this volume. Dates are included to facilitate orientation. Italics and punctuation are as the German edition of 1977. Additions are set in square brackets.

In the notes on Lecture 2 of 5 February, a quotation taken from Lecture 6 of the Vienna lecture cycle *The Inner Nature of the Human Being and Life between Death and a New Birth* (Collected Works CW153), has been inserted. This quotation does not appear in notes taken at the Zurich lectures but does, however, appear in the essay 'Key Points of the Social Question', Chapter 4, as also in a series of lectures dating from the subsequent weeks and months. In the notes relating to Lecture 3 of 10 February, the last three paragraphs refer to Woodrow Wilson's essay 'The New Freedom', which was published in German in Munich in 1914.

The conceptual model for the public lecture of 8 March can be found in the Rudolf Steiner archives under reference number 5462/63.

***

I. The true dimensions of the social challenge in terms of essential living needs and researched by spiritual-scientific methods.

II. Attempts at resolving social issues and needs—as demanded by life, which are congruent with reality and seen from spiritual-scientific perspectives.

III. Zealotry and realism in social thinking and will.
IV. Evolving social thinking and will—central issues for contemporary humanity.

From a *viewpoint bearing the hallmarks of reality, grounded in real life* and viewed from spiritual-scientific perspectives, whose aim is *prejudice-free* thinking and research. These lectures aim to give expression to a *multi-faceted compilation* of humanity's *real and present needs* in the field of social challenge. Their focus = [*sic*] aims to make factual that only such an iteration can generate understanding of real-life demands in this context and—instead of misconceptions, impractical goals and evolution-hindering debates—to create productive work in this field. Only such means of observing can conceptually unite intrinsic consciousness of freedom with exigencies of communal social living and be realizable in action.

[Lecture 1, Zurich 3 February 1919]
The true dimensions of the social challenge, based on spiritual-scientific research into human needs

1. Catastrophic times have brought forces buried deep in social living to the surface, playing into the causes of the war.
2. People talk about social issues in isolation, globalizing them. They are not detached from real life. They are only segregated because the other two spheres of the societal organism with which they are connected are atrophied. Nowhere do the true dimensions of societal issues emerge. Demands emerge. But the creative forces for resolution are missing.
3. Those emergent demands arise from various quarters: from economic life = does production match demand? From a feeling of human dignity = can human labour be allowed to be considered a commodity? Re understanding social community: bridges have been burnt. There is no understanding across and between classes. Only class struggle is trusted. Scientific thinking modalities can only comprehend purely economic life. Spiritual-cultural life has become mere ideology to the proletariat.
   Supremacy of capital. Dependency. Crises. Production for profit. Socialism is *like a religion.*

Socialism as a doctrine because life lacks social impetus. Social stimuli were (in their own way) more widespread and accessible in days gone by than today.
Socialism considers itself a 'scientific doctrine' and a world view.

1. The economy determines historic conditions. Everything else—rights, conventions, morality—are ideological super-constructs. Slavery, feudalism, private capitalism.
2. Workers create profit.
3. All history is the history of class warfare.

It was just when a class previously excluded from education edged into learning that education lost its motivating power. Religious nuances in learning were no longer absorbed. This is because earlier these religious nuances became incapable of exerting any influence on natural-scientific thinking.

1. The disaster of war revealed the urgency of core social issues everywhere. This had pre-existed in proletarian consciousness. Yet it led to avoiding any solution. You have to be in a position to observe psychologically what lives in proletarian psyches.
2. The 'scientific' nature of proletarian class consciousness. This is evidence that the ascendant proletarian movement is connected with the way in which proletarians learnt to think i.e. 'scientifically'. This inclined them to focus solely on economics. They became familiar with the essentials of commodity production.
3. This led to the assumption that their applied research was informed by economic imperatives. Yet this entailed human labour being ensnared within the capitalist production process as a commodity.
4. Spiritual-intellectual culture became ideology for the proletarian personality.
5. This is responsible for obscuring what ensues from life's basic needs: the onward evolution of humanity itself. Essentials of the social organism.

Play = occupation by choice. *Work* = out of necessity and duty, the will of others.

Reducing working hours is the stated aim but its underlying function is liberation from long-term dependency.

If spiritual life is intermixed with both the other societal spheres, the latter are denied the influx that enlivens their potential.

Economic life is subject to laws that continually cause the social organism to stagnate.

The true dimensions of the social challenge, based on spiritual-scientific research into human needs

1. How the origin and progression of social issues were factors to be reckoned with.
2. Something burdens parts of Europe like tragedy: people were faced with the need to judge what could be turned into action = one can barely concede that such a verdict resulted.
3. *One* thing saw the light of day in the proletarian movement: they disowned thinking and yet are primarily a thought-based movement.

[on the opposite page]

Only those able to transform their opinions will be equal to the challenges of the time.

The *old programmes* persist: but the facts have changed so fundamentally that people insulate themselves as if mummified within those facts.

Life constantly poses new challenges and demands.

The catastrophe of war is like a final act in which human initiative has run out. What is left will require a completely new assessment.

[text continues]

4. But this points to intentions quite different from those expressed in thoughts.
   Central for those capable of observing life, who have themselves lived among proletarians, are workers and their 'class consciousness'.
5. But 'class consciousness' only serves as a front that masks. It is in truth pan-human consciousness in a form prompted by the machine within the capitalist economy.
6. There is ultimately no economic antagonism between bourgeoisie and proletariat, just a lack of understanding based on other factors. The bourgeois citizen sees Hauptmann's 'The Weavers'. [Play about Silesian weavers in revolt against the machine age. Transl.] What s/he perceives is her/his own misconception.

7. A worker, isolated at a machine, a unit yoked to capitalism, struggles with modern thinking (e.g. Marx).
8. This thinking has lost all conceptual momentum to nurture empathy with humanity as a whole. It only understands the economic system.
9. Such thinking has never manifested as an independent force. It has been subsumed into state structures.
10. Hence within proletarian thinking there is *ideology*.
11. Opinions on the fundamental call for labour *not to be* commodified. This question put to politics. Herein *inequality* is experienced.
12. Capital/ism falsifies a person's relationship with the economic process. It is the economic process that brings about capital growth. Human beings are *powerless* in the face of this. It is a betrayal of fraternity or brotherliness.

1	Spiritual	=	Love for the matter or activity in hand
2	Political	=	Will to do right, justice, law
3	Economic	=	Desire for use (purpose)
			(Interest in usefulness, value of utility)

[On page opposite point 12]

Capitalism aims for value-addition, profit. This is the root of the belief in its *other effects*...

Hardship, misery and misfortune do not essentially originate in human beings—they can only emanate from conditions—Proletarians know this (possibly unconsciously)—One cannot really rejoice about one's body; but one suffers pain when it is out of order—Anyone who maintains that hardship is a necessary evil will not be taken seriously by the proletariat. *Healthiness* hinders the social organism but *does not hinder* one in unfolding happiness and joy. The body economic can only be disrupted by the other bodies or spheres.

[Lecture 2, 5 February 1919]
Attempts at solving social issues from a spiritual-scientific perspective aligned with life and congruent with reality

1. Social thinking has lately focused on economic and technical progress. This ignores the fact that a form of life and its associated needs have been activated and cannot be guided onto the right trajectory by an economic system alone.

[On the opposite page]

Incentives or stimuli unilaterally originating in a single set of living conditions should not be given credence. G*enuine* living needs should be the decisive factor. What is the use of a single class imprinting the entire social organism in its own image? This elicits the very opposite effect, which is that another class emerges to detrimental effect.

[Text continues]

2. The capitalist economic model has eliminated from its purview every impulse originating in life's fundamentals *except* the economy itself.
3. The socialist mindset current among proletarians has lost all faith that an existence worthy of human beings is attainable for itself in any other way than through a system of purely economic relationships.
4. The economy is only one sphere of the overall social organism. If people are placed in a life governed solely by economic principles, their essential being withers.
5. How the other two components of the social organism are being *enslaved* by private sector capitalism is being ignored.
6. Those other two component spheres must be freed. While learning from observing the human organism, basic social needs also have to be viewed correctly. Only taking account of laws you assume you have recognized in a human organism and believing them to be transferable onto the social organism just proves you incapable of assessing society in terms of *its own* needs.
7. How to observe a human organism.
8. How to observe the social organism: in terms of its natural foundations, it resembles the human organism and is subject to similar laws that relate to its natural origins, much like the way in which a human organism is related to its natural talents. Natural talents or gifts cannot be directly elicited through learning. A social contrivance cannot alter the fact that labour costs for banana production relate to those of wheat production roughly 400:3 [*sic*]. A social order cannot alter the fact that German wheat yields 7 or 8 times its outlay in sowing costs, in Chile this is some 12 times, in Northern Mexico 17 times, in Peru 20 times, in Southern Mexico 25-35 times. But if the social organism is structured according to its inherent laws, the production

of a given region will follow similarly to the way in which giftedness emerges from a human organism if rightly treated by the education system.

9. The social organism is only *healthy* once its independent constituent components are structured as follows:

   1. The economy connects human beings with their nature-based foundations. A semi-personal relationship needs to exist between humans and original factors of production.

2. The legislative-rights sphere where all people are treated as equal before the law and in which completely impersonal relationships must pertain.	This is the field in which healthy democracy can prove its efficacy. The now outdated liberalism did not understand this. This sphere cannot deliver such laws as pertain in the spiritual-cultural and the economic spheres.
3. The spiritual sphere, which leaves each individual person free in terms of their personal development. Here the most personal ethos must be able to operate.	Its *content* has been contaminated, made toxic by desire for that which does not belong to its content: Position—or wishing to enforce a tendency or trend = Party: conservative, liberal etc. Who has erected barricades around the spiritual-cultural sphere to prevent this from happening?

10. These spheres must collaborate in real life but not as a single abstract unit. Representatives of each sphere must keep sharp watch that their independence is not compromised but safeguarded. The regulation of employment conditions must not become muddled by absorbing economic elements into the second sphere, thereby causing the value of human labour to be commodified. The economy must only be concerned with the production

of goods, their circulation and consumption. The political sphere will only be concerned with everything in which all human beings are equal. The spiritual-cultural sphere will be concerned with all things freedom-related—with all individual initiative that can only unfold and flourish in freedom.

11. Experience of these views during the catastrophe of war. What is being talked about. No bridge has been found between theoretical comprehension and practical will. It had been hoped that bitter experience might have produced initiative in this vein.
12. People shy away from what reality demands due *either* to thinking it radical (they want to heal society in face of phenomena such as e.g. sexual maturity). *Or* this model is considered to be the outpourings of impractical idealism.
13. Some have found that this model is thought to apply only to internal matters. But it is a foundational blueprint for external conditions in state arenas. These need to separately challenge each other, mitigating with their qualities any drawbacks caused to or by any other sphere. Confused societal intermixing must lead to conflict and disaster and the greatest of these began in 1914.

In Vienna:

> This tendency will grow ever stronger and more widespread to a point where it prompts its own destruction. Those able to fathom social life in spiritual terms see spiritual ulcers breaking out on every side. This is the enormous cultural worry among those able to plumb existence. It is something terrible and oppressive. Even when all enthusiasm for spiritual science might otherwise have been suppressed—like suppressing even what would otherwise allow one to open one's mouth to speak in favour of spiritual science—it would be like seeking a panacea for the world while screaming against what is already so aggressively in the ascendant and becoming ever more powerful. If the social organism continues to evolve as it has thus far, cultural destruction will ensue which will affect society in ways that replicate cancer in the human body.

[Lecture 3, 10 February 1919]
III. Zealotry and realism in social thinking and will
Notes:

1. *Freedom* can only thrive in a cultural-spiritual milieu evolving completely autonomously. Freely unfolding forces rely on thinking that results from a self-regulating intellectual life ...

2. All specific instances can follow on from structuring the social organism nature-compatibly: organizing the economic sphere associatively. Humans' relationship with their natural foundations enables coalitions and associations that are capable of dealing with each other constructively. Here *value creation* is critical and *contracts* are pivotal.

   Legal relationships: Relationships between people are fundamental. Legislation is the determining factor. It then follows that those who act for the prosperity and flourishing of others in society 'rightfully' have rights. Power is not the decisive factor, but the degree to which a person's exertions influence the social organism.

   Individual spiritual-intellectual culture: The decisive factor here is the *freedom* with which soul-spiritual gifts are able to unfold.

   The logic of reality dictates: Tax system, significance of money, relation of capital/ism to money etc.

   Determining factors:

   In the economy: the system of *contracts* ensuing from opportunity.

   In the political sphere: the system of public *rights*.

   In the spiritual sphere: *free competition* among talents, evolved forces and activities [*sic*].

Land: A genuine relationship must exist between land and those working it. But this relationship cannot be allowed to harm the societal organism as a whole.

Anything that places increase in land yields below the right to such yield must be ditched: a right to mortgages must be a priority ...

Capital cannot lie in value (mortgage bonds, mortgages) for which high land prices serve as collateral security.

Wealth accumulation that fails to link such wealth with the social process will inevitably cause harm. If a person has used their *ingenuity* on inventing a machine, it will represent not only *their* inventiveness but the incentive motivation of the entire community.

Labour may only flow into the economy once i.e. *after* its extent and limits have been defined in terms of rights legislation. A branch of production demanding unsustainable levels of labour input should as little be considered permissible as one whose raw materials are too expensive to be viable.

Where does zealous spinning or fanaticism originate? In disjunctively cutting loose one branch of thinking *from another.*

Mercantilism is devoid of all consciousness as to how states becoming centres of trade impact on the economy (Colbert 1619–1687, Cromwell, Friedrich Wilhelm the first, Frederick the Great). Countries being closed to one another.

The Physiocrats: Economic life governed entirely by laws of nature, which ought to have free rein.

Quesnay:

1. Productivity of land
2. Non-productive trade and industry. Its only tax: agricultural income tax.
3. Artificial proliferation of money is useless
4. *Laissez faire, laissez aller* (permissiveness and slackness)

Much may appear correct in the above view—what causes it to be inadequate?

Taxation will only be correctly aligned if you assume that:

The moment I and my activity intervene in the social organism, I put on the market something for which I have the community to thank: so I have to pay tax. If I pay for a product of industry or a trade benefit, I have to pay tax for the option of including myself in the social organism. In either case, the *beneficiary* has to pay tax. Doesn't this lead to pressure on prices? Only when the producer can afford to be pressurized—but not when this is not the case.

[Lecture 3, 10 February 1919]
Zealotry and realism in social thinking and will

1. You always have to come back to this: the mutual misunderstandings between previously leading classes and newly aspiring sectors is one of the greatest hindrances in present social living. In the former coteries, 'proletarian thinking' is not remotely understood. Due

to their habitual thought patterns, they have no means of grasping how such thinking has become criticism of those steeped lifelong in bourgeois civic society. But it is just criticism and doesn't represent any intention to act on it. 'What happens will become evident once the proletariat have gained mastery.'

2. You have to reach an awareness that: recent habitual thinking tropes do not generate any thoughts capable of grasping the web of actual economic factors and forces—in most cases such thinking becomes mired in zealotry and spin ...
3. This irrational, fanatical thinking gives rise to isolated Utopias; but worse than setting up Utopias is a utopian *mode* of thinking. It is precisely those purporting to be 'practical folk' who have recently espoused utopian thinking and claimed it as their own. They focus primarily on notions of pursuing happiness.
4. Modern thinking has lost the ability to drill down to reality: a matter of releasing the inner psychic forces to which full reality can reveal itself.
5. To this end, 'spiritual life' has to be placed on a footing of complete *freedom*—including permeating everyday life. Freedom can never be instated as long as the political sphere oversees or controls this domain.
6. Society's legislative arm cannot be an economist. Nor, conversely, can it allow itself to be abused by the economic sector. This would necessitate favouring *itself* as legislator. In this sphere, people have to work in their capacity as human beings. Fundamental law: a person can only work *for others.*

[On the opposite page]

This sphere must be capable of restricting the economy. It ought to *enliven* it = *it* works such that that it *exploits people.* It can never make people happy—it must be possible for people to tear themselves away from it. The *basis of legislature* is not power, but what is beneficial for the general public. A person with the will to carry out something grounded in law is accorded the right to place this initiative in the service of society as a whole.

As regards foreign policy, external politics, global war has proved that internationalism cannot be achieved if it is overwhelmingly based on economic foundations.

It has been said that *peoples or nations* cannot be sold off like commodities—this is first and foremost a human concern.
[text continues]

7. Within the economy the link between human being and preconditions of production, trade and consumption must prevail. Labour, for instance, plays into this and can only disengage from the circulation of goods if it both fundamentally underlies it and co-determines it.

How elemental world events will determine economic intentions; Turkish forces appear in Constantinople [Istanbul]; *Europe's economies should cease their eastward expansion.*

Wilson said: With the discovery of America it became possible for Europe's populations to 'engage in a new historical experiment'.

According to Wilson: 'Human freedom consists in correctly dovetailing the coincidence of human interests, trade and powers.'

Economic activity requires human beings to adapt to fulfilling the interests of society as a whole: the suspension of freedom. If a ship sails downwind, it can move *freely*. If it sails to windward, it is trapped, beating against the wind and making no headway. In that sense it is only free in being a component within a context. If it possessed consciousness, it could only *believe* itself to be free as long as did not notice that it had been divested of its freedom so as not to be impeded by its context. Proletarians could *believe* themselves to be free if their activity were aligned with—adapted to—the interests of the entrepreneur. But they stop living in this belief as soon as they become aware that doing so is counter to *their own* interests. A ship can only be considered 'free' if at any given moment it is *not* bound to obey the wind, but can change its course despite the wind working against it. Proletarians have to position themselves such that the capitalist has an interest in using their *leisure* just as s/he uses their *efforts* or *labour*. Capital has to produce something, which lacks substance without workers' leisure. This is counteracted if the capital has a chance to be something in its own right and is not forced to *flow into* the social organism. You have to be induced to *spend*, to *expend* your capital (to *purchase*). That only applies if in life you become impoverished without spending, if without expenditure your income dries up. An entrepreneur has to need workers not only for their ability to produce but for their lives—s/he has to need them as consumers of what they produce. But this entails an association between consumers, producers, society, brotherliness or fraternity which unites consumers of a product line; and as this is not immediately possible within the circumstances of present humanity, it signals *a system of associations* ...

[Zurich, 12 February 1919]
Notes:

In the *evolving social thinking and will*, it is not a matter of economics but of the human personality's influence...

Even at a soul level, the belief persists that individual human beings are embedded in society. Among the proletariat this embeddedness is made attributable to impersonal factors in economic life—nobody wants to be reliant on other people = spawns purely economic thinking within bourgeois intellectual circles: proletarians have embraced this view—: but they want to further politicize economic life instead of *freeing* it from the politicization that has already set in.

What is the significance of blue-collar labour?

Notes for the public lecture on 8 March 1919 in Zurich

1. When this lecture was announced, some may have wondered from where the speaker wishing to address them hails. Judging by the answers received, it might be concluded that enough had been heard from this quarter.
2. I am not going to talk about *agreement*, because I agree with those who do not become involved in the way much is discussed just for the sake of agreement.
3. For more than half a century, those who had previously occupied leading positions could see how a movement was taking shape which unified within its ranks those who were calling out in their direction: 'You have until recently had control over everything existing in terms of social structures. You created it. But we are saying to you: this cannot continue.' Yet those calling for change met with little understanding. And now there is the so-called World War. It has shown that movement in a new light. It has also shown its inability to continue trading in the societal thinking constructed by once-leading classes themselves. The social movement in disastrous times of war.
4. Movements going under widely varying names sprang up within those leading classes, those pre-eminent echelons. But another sector which, due to its background, was also ready to campaign for a social movement could extend no trust towards the former movements. They felt obliged to tell them that they were thinking in terms inherited from their class. The thinking required to heal society was not to be found among the very sector which had colluded in the shaping of those conditions. Only those *not* infected by their prejudices nor indoctrinated by what their social standing taught them could imagine what needed to be done.
5. How these circumstances came about. Contemporary proletarians have been developing their own science. Pre-eminent circles have only slowly become accustomed to some things.
6. The question as to the significance of human labour underlies everything to such an extent that it is more a question of pan-human dignity. Labour as a commodity.

7. This is the only arena in which this issue can rightly be addressed. It has to be understood that labour can never be a commodity. Because it has been reduced to a commodity, we are mired in *a life-sized deception.* Workers see themselves facing capitalist trading operations and an economy that makes a commodity of their labour.
8. In order to keep this life-sized deception alive, it has often been said that throne and altar must maintain the social order's status quo. But will it be to oppressors' benefit if machine and office take over?
9. Will something viable thrive if a different economic system is grafted onto the framework of the state?

9a. Trust will be extended towards organizing the economy.
Sole question: How will it be *socialized?*

10. The only remedy is to reconfigure the social organism. No blending, melding nor amalgamating. The following facts have to be taken on board: a spiritual sphere will only thrive once it is set free. State-legislature, rights: only once it is not determined by the interests of the economy. Economy: only when it cannot amass power because it is self-dependent.
11. Capital can only work effectively in a freed spiritual sphere. Because it has not become what it is thanks to the economy, nor to the legislative sphere, but due to the capacities of individual people. Labour can only be regulated by the legislative-rights element of the state, because it falls prey to coercive power if governed solely by the economy.
12. Crucial to understand that *rethinking* is vital...

Notes

1 Workers' College: Between 1899 and 1904 Rudolf Steiner taught at this college for workers' education founded in 1891 by the Social Democrat Wilhelm Liebknecht. Firstly, in the faculty of History and Speech Training, later also in the Science department, see Rudolf Steiner's *Autobiography*, Collected Works no. 28, Dornach 1962, Chapter 28 and Rudolf Steiner *Briefe II 1892–1902* ('Letters II 1892–1902'), Dornach 1953, as also Johanna Mücke & Alwin Rudolph, *Erinnerungen an Rudolf Steiner und seine Tätigkeit an der Arbeiterbildungsschule in Berlin 1899–1904* ('Recollections of Rudolf Steiner and his Activities at the Workers' Education College in Berlin 1899–1904'), Basel 1955.

2 Karl Marx (1818–1883). The foundational theoretical basis inaugurating 'Scientific Socialism' and 'Dialectical Materialism' can be found in his *Early Writings*, culminating as *The Communist Manifesto* of 1848. See particularly *Critique of Hegelian Political Philosophy* of 1841–42, *The Holy Family* of 1844–45 and *German Ideology* of 1845–46.

3 Friedrich Engels (1821–1895), co–founder with Karl Marx of Scientific Socialism and Dialectical Materialism. This latter was actively popularized by him. After Marx's death he published Volumes II (1885) and III (1894) of *Das Kapital* or *Capital*.

4 *... a mighty revolution:* Compare Rudolf Steiner's *The Education of the Child in Light of Spiritual Science* (1907) in *Luzifer–Gnosis. Grundlegende Aufsätze zur Anthroposophie und Berichte aus der Zeitschrift 'Luzifen' und 'Lucifer–Gnosis' 1903–1908*, ('Foundational Essays on Anthroposophy and Reports in the journal *Lucifer* and *Lucifer–Gnosis*, 1903–1908'), Collected Works Dornach 1960, CW 34.

5 *When Galileo and Giordano Bruno were being condemned:* Spiritual–historical evolution at the turning point of a new age, alongside Galileo (1564–1642) and Giordano Bruno (1548–1600) Copernicus (1473–1543), Kepler (1571–1630) and Francis Bacon (1561–1626) should be mentioned. Rudolf Steiner describes them in detail in his book *The Riddles of Philosophy* (1914), Collected Works Dornach 1960, CW 18.

6 The programmes here referred to include: The *Eisenach Programme*, set up in August 1869 on the occasion of the founding of the

Social–Democratic Workers' Party by W. Liebknecht and A. Bebel. The *Gothar Programme* of May 1875 on the occasion of Lassalle amalgamating this Workers' Party with the roughly equally strong All–Germany Workers' Union, and:

The *Erfurt Programme* of October 1891, formed by Kausky, on the occasion of the re–deployment of The Social Democratic Party of Germany as a member of the group founded two years previously, the Second Internationale.

The first two of these programmes were still strongly influenced by Lassalle's peaceful path towards solving the socialist issue with state aid—at whose midst were demands to scrap existing pay structures and the instatement of political equality among all people—and in this way the more belligerent class–warfare elements gained ground. Because of this, Kausky designed—for the Erfurt political convention—a purely Marxist programme, about which Rudolf Steiner said that it was 'intended to make Marxism the official view of the proletariat'. Compare: Rudolf Steiner's lecture on 'The History of the Social Movement' in: *Neugestaltung des sozialen Organismus* ('Restructuring the Social Organism'), Collected Works Dornach 1963, CW330/331.

7 Rudolf Steiner outlined the threefold nature of the human organism in the chapter on 'The Physical and Spiritual Dependence of the Human Being' in his book *Riddles of the Soul* which appeared in 1917, Collected Works CW 21.

8 Albert Schäffle (1831–1903), political economist and sociologist, minister in Württemberg's regional parliament 1862–65 and Austrian Minister of Trade in 1871, who compiled, i.a. *Bau und Leben des sozialen Körpers* ('The Construction and Life of the Body Social'), 1875–78, 4 vols. 2nd edition 1896, 2 vols.

9 C.H. Meray, *Weltmutation. Schöpfungsgesetze über Krieg und Frieden und die Geburt einer neuen Zivilisation* ('World Mutation. Laws of Creation regarding War and Peace and the Birth of a New Civilisation'), Zurich 1918.

10 Compare with Carl Jentsch, *Volkswirtschaftslehre. Grundbegriffe und Grundsätze der Volkswirtschaft* ('Doctrine of Popular Economy: Fundamental Concepts and Objectives of Popular Economy'), 4th edition, Leipzig 1918, p.64.

11 *Freedom, Equality, Fraternity*: Compare with this the Stuttgart lecture by Rudolf Steiner 'Freedom of Spirit, Equality of Rights, Fraternity in the Economy' (18 June 1919) in 'Reshaping the Social Organism', see above, and also the lecture held on 15 September 1919 in Berlin 'Realising the Ideals of Freedom, Equality and Fraternity' in *Freedom of Thought and Societal Forces*, Collected Works CW 333, Dornach 1971.

12 Between Central and Western powers—after concluding the truce of Compiègne—no genuine peace accords were reached. The 'Paris Peace Conference' which opened in Versailles was merely an assembly of delegated proxies of the 27 Entente states for the purpose of agreeing conditions to be imposed on Central powers.
The International Socialists' Conference took place in Bern, Switzerland, 3–10 February 1919.

13 See Rudolf Steiner's lecture on 'The History of the Social Movement' in *Geschichte der sozialen Bewegung* ('Restructuring the Social Organism'), CW 330/331. In that lecture, Steiner describes the French Socialist Charles Fourier (1772–1837) and Louis Blanc (1813–1882) and also the French philosopher and 'religious socialist' Claude Henry de Saint–Simon (1760–1825) as 'Utopian Socialists.'

14 Erich Ludendorff (1865–1937), between 1916–18 First Quartermaster General of German Forces, he also gained far–reaching influence in politics and economics (Sturz Bethmann Hollwegs). In 1923 Ludendorff took part in Hitler's *coup d'état* and, with his wife Matilde, founded the 'Peoples' Christian Union of Tannenberg' [a village in N. Poland, site of a German victory over Russians in 1914—Transl.]

15 The German Society for Ethical Culture was founded at the instigation of W. Foerster and Georg von Gizycki in 1892 in Berlin. See Rudolf Steiner *Autobiography*, Chapter 17 and both essays on this society in *Gesammelte Aufsätze zur Kultur—und Zeitgeschichte 1887–1901* ('Collected Essays on Contemporary Cultural History 1887–1901'), Collected Works CW 31, Dornach 1966, pp.164 and 169 ff.

16 See J.W. Goethe's *Faust,* part II, scene in the laboratory.

17 In his work *The Philosophy of Freedom—Outline of a Modern World View—Results of Soul Observation using the Methods of Natural Science* which appeared in 1894, Rudolf Steiner created the fundamental preconditions for a spiritual–scientific view of the world. The new edition mentioned

appeared in 'substantially extended and revised' form in 1918. Collected Works, CW 4, Dornach 1973.

18 See Karl Marx *Das Kapital*, vol. 1, section 2, Chapter 4, 'Buying and Selling Labour' and section 3, Chapter 5 'Employment and Exploitative Processes'.

19 It was not Stephenson but Humphrey Potter who, in 1713, was tasked with manually operating both valves of a Newcomen–Cawley–Savary atmospheric steam engine, where power is created by suction rather than pressure. Separate condensers were then unknown. Steam condensation still took place in the cylinders themselves. Potter had to alternately allow steam–and–water in by injection, and water, which condensed the steam in the cylinder back to condensate (water). He invented a mechanism to do this automatically.

20 Ludwig Laistner (1845–1896), literary adviser to the Cotta publishing company and bookshop. See Rudolf Steiner's *Autobiography*, Chapter 15.

21 Fundamental Social Law: this 'soziale Hauptgesetz', informed by spiritual–scientific observation, is expressed as follows:
'The potential for the entirety of a group of people working together to thrive is increased the less single individuals take for themselves the proceeds of their efforts, which means that the more of those proceeds can be meted out among their co–workers and the more their own needs are fulfilled by the efforts of those others.' From the essay 'Spiritual Science and Social Question' in *Lucifer Gnosis*—separate publication of this essay, Dornach 1977.

22 Further to this example of being a tailor, see Rudolf Steiner's *Rethinking Economics*, Collected Works, Dornach 1965, CW 340 (particularly lectures 3, 4 and 7); also *Nationalökonomisches Seminar* ('Political Economy Seminar'), CW 341 Dornach 1973.

23 *The ancient Platonic concept..*: Described in Plato's *Politeia* ('The State').

24 Karl von Clausewitz (1780–1831), Prussian Major General and militaria writer, editor of the 8–volume *Vom Kriege* ('On War'); the sentence used here is taken from volume 1.

25 What Rudolf Steiner is here alluding to is his *An das deutsche Volk und an die Kulturwelt* ('Appeal to the People of Germany and to World Culture' [or the cultural world. Transl.]) which was printed and distributed in February 1919 as a flyer bearing the signatures of numerous personali-

ties active in political, economic and cultural life. See also Rudolf Steiner 'Die Kernpunkte der sozialen Frage...', p. 157–162 ('Key Points of the Social Issue') and *Nachrichten der Rudolf Steiner–Nachlaßverwaltung* ('News from the Rudolf Steiner Estate Administration') nos. 24/25 Easter 1969, pp.21–23.

26 See also Karl Marx 'Theses on Feuerbach', no. 11, literally: 'Philosophers have just interpreted the world variously; it is a matter of changing it.' (After Karl Marx, *Frühschriften*, 'Early Writings', published by S. Landshut, Stuttgart 1968, p.341.)

27 At the opening of the new Workers' Education Institute in Spandau on 12 June 1902 Rosa Luxemburg gave a lecture on the theme of 'Science and the Workers' Struggle'. Following on from this, Rudolf Steiner addressed the same topic, see Beiträge zur Rudolf Steiner Gesamtausgabe ('Contributions on Rudolf Steiner's Collected Works') no. 36, turn of the years 1971–72.

28 Schäffle and Meray. Ibid.

29 Setting prices: Compare with Rudolf Steiner's elaboration in the *Rethinking Economics* course and *Nationalökonomisches Seminar* ('Political Economy Seminar').

30 Karl Giskra (1820–1879) who was 1867–1870 Minister of the Interior.

31 Nikolai Berdyáyev (1874–1948) and see following endnote.

32 Richard Avenarius (1843–1896), Philosopher and Empirical Knowledge Theoretician, who lived latterly in Zurich and founded a positivist philosophy—in his *Kritik der reinen Erfahrung* ('Critique of Pure Experience'), 2 volumes, 1888–1900, 2nd edition 1908—which he termed 'Emperiocriticism' or Empirical Criticism, and in which he describes individuals' experience as being dependent on their environments. Lenin opposed this Emperiocriticism in his work *Materialism and Empirio–criticism*, in which he waxes polemical against the empiricism contained in the Marxist doctrine posited there.

33 Friedrich Adler (1836–1916) leader of the Austrian Social Democrats, one of the theoreticians of Austro–Marxism, follower of Emperiocriticism, he tried to amplify Marxism with 'Machist' philosophy (see below). On 21 October 1916 he shot the Austrian Prime Minister, Count Stürgkh, was condemned to death but freed in 1918. He was later to lead the Nationalist Socialist Workers' International.

34 Ernst Mach (1838–1916), Austro–Czech Physicist and Philosopher, one of the founders of Emperiocriticism; within his theory of knowledge he revived the views of Berkeley and Hume. His epistemic views greatly influenced theoretical physics (Mach Number, M or Ma) and were expanded by the Vienna Circle (of Logical Empiricism). Among much else, in 1883 he wrote *Die Mechanik in ihrer Entwicklung* ('Analysis of Sensation and the Relationship between Physical and Psyche'); *Beiträge zur Analyse der Empfindungen* ('Knowledge and Error: Sketches for a Psychology of Research') in 1905; *Die Leitgedanken meiner naturwissenschaftlichen Erkenntnislehre* ('Leading Thoughts of my Scientific Theory of Knowledge'), 1919.

35 ... *official philosophy of Bolshevism*: Here Rudolf Steiner is drawing on an essay by Nikolai A. Berdyáyev on *Die politische und die philosophische Wahrheit* ('Political and Philosophical Truth') appearing in Elias Hurwicz's work *Rußlands politische Seele* ('Russia's Political Soul'), published in 1918 in Berlin. This essay had already appeared in Russia in 1909 in the collection entitled *Vietchi.* The German edition included this text: 'Then they [Russian Intelligence, publisher's note] turned to the hard–to–digest Avenarius because his "purest", most abstract philosophy had—without his knowledge or fault—suddenly been presented as a philosophy of Bolshevism.' See also Rudolf Steiner's *Die soziale Grundforderung unserer Zeit. In geänderter Zeitlage* ('Fundamental Social Demands of our Time—in the changed conditions of the present'), Collected Works, CW 186, Dornach 1963. Lectures 9 and 10 and Lecture 3 in *Geisteswissenschaftliche Behandlung sozialer und pädagogischer Fragen* ('Handling Social and Pedagogical Issues Spiritual–Scientifically'), Collected Works, CW 192, Dornach 1964.

36 Rosa Luxemburg (1871–1919), socialist politician. She belonged to representatives of the radical stream among Polish Social Democrats (later Communist Party of Germany). At the Social Democratic Party school in Berlin she taught Marxist Political Economy. During World War I, due to her call for opposition to the war, she found herself almost constantly in prison. In 1917, with Karl Liebknecht, she founded the Spartacus League and, at the end of 1918, the Communist Party. In the January 1919 revolt she and Karl Liebknecht were shot without trial by Government troops.

37 Henri Bergson (1859–1941), French philosopher and Professor at Paris's Collège de France, his philosophy stemmed from a critique of Kant's Time Theory. According to Bergson, time is—in its essential nature—duration, perpetuity. Duration and reality itself can be apprehended by Intuition. See also Rudolf Steiner's *Riddles of Philosophy* and *Aus dem mitteleuropäischen Geistesleben* ('On Central European Spirituality'), Collected Works CW 65, Dornach 1962. Henri Bergson wrote i.a. *Zeit und Freiheit* ('Time and Freedom') in 1889, *Materie und Gedächtnis* ('Matter and Memory') in 1896, *Die schöpferische Entwicklung* ('Creative Evolution') in 1907 and *Denken und schöpferisches Werden* ('Thinking and Creative Becoming') in 1934.

38 Arthur Schopenhauer (1788–1860), philosopher. To Schopenhauer the world is fundamentally *will* and *idea* or concept. The body is will objectified. Everything conceivably capable of being conceptualized to do with knowledge is an object in relation to a subject, is the view of the viewer, and is an idea. His main work is *Die Welt als Wille und Vorstellung* ('The World as Will and Idea'), 1819, final edition 1859, 2 volumes. See also Rudolf Steiner's Introduction to *Arthur Schopenhauers sämtliche Werke in zwölf Bände* ('Arthur Schopenhauer's Collected Works in Twelve Volumes'), Cotta Library of World Literature, Stuttgart 1894.

39 Franz Mehring (1846–1919), politician and writer. He was one of the leading figures in the German Workers' Union, acting i.a. in defence of Social Democracy against Bismarck. He wrote *Geschichte der deutschen Sozialdemokratie* ('History of German Social Democracy') in 1877 (liberal–bourgeois), 4 volumes of the same title in 1897 (socialist), *Die Lessing–Legende* ('The Lessing Legend') in 1893 and *Karl Marx* in 1918.

40 Ferdinand Lassalle (1825–1864), founder of the Social Democratic movement in Germany. In his defence speech in Berlin's Criminal Court (when facing charges of inciting non–property–owning classes to hatred and publicly inciting the destruction of property) on the topic of 'Science and Workers' he said, amongst much else: 'Precisely this determines the size of our times: *carrying out* what dim centuries gone by would not even have considered it possible *to think: bringing science to the people!*' From *Ferdinand Lassalle's Reden und Schriften* ('Ferdinand Lassalle's Speeches and Writings'), Berlin 1893.

41 Carl Vogt (1817–1895) Natural scientist, researcher and active Democrat, member of the Frankfurt Parliament. Identified by Karl Marx in his

polemic paper 'Mr Vogt' (1860) as being a paid–up secret agent of—and apologist for—Louis Bonaparte. He wrote i.a. *Physiologische Briefe für Gebildete aller Stände* ('Physiological Letters for the Educated of all Echelons of Society'), Stuttgart–Tübingen 1857.

42 Ludwig Büchner (1824–1899), doctor and philosopher, brother of Georg Büchner (dramatist and revolutionary) exponent of unconstrained materialism and Darwinism. He wrote *Kraft und Stoff* ('Power and Matter') in 1855 and *Darwinismus und Sozialismus* ('Darwinism and Socialism') in 1894.

43 Rudolf Steiner's father was a telegraphist for Southern Austrian Railways. See his *Autobiography*, Chapter 1.

Rudolf Steiner's Collected Works

The German Edition of Rudolf Steiner's Collected Works (the *Gesamtausgabe* [GA], published by Rudolf Steiner Verlag, Dornach, Switzerland) will be completed in the year 2025. The works are organized either by type of work (written, spoken, artistic creations), chronology, audience (public or other), or subject (education, art, etc.). For ease of comparison, the Collected Works in English (CW), listed below, follows the German organization and numbering.

The volumes that have so far been published in the English Collected Works edition appear *in italics with their published titles*; all other volumes, including those that have appeared in editions other than the CW, are set in Roman type with *literal translations* of the German titles. Published English titles are not necessarily the same as the German.

This list is current as of the date of this volume's publication.

A. Written Works

I. Writings 1884–1925

CW 1	Introductions and Selected Commentary on Goethe's Natural-scientific Writings
CW 1a–e	Goethe's Natural-scientific Writings
CW 1f	Editorial Afterwords to Goethe's Natural-scientific Writings in the Weimar Edition (1891–1896)
CW 2	*Goethe's Theory of Knowledge: An Outline of the Epistemology of His Worldview*
CW 3	Truth and Science
CW 4	The Philosophy of Freedom
CW 4a	Documents to "The Philosophy of Freedom"
CW 5	Friedrich Nietzsche, A Fighter against His Own Time

CW 6	Goethe's Worldview
CW 7	Mysticism at the Dawn of Modern Spiritual Life and Its Relationship with Modern Worldviews
CW 8	*Christianity as Mystical Fact and the Mysteries of Antiquity*
CW 9	Theosophy: An Introduction into Supersensible World Knowledge and Human Purpose
CW 10	How Does One Attain Knowledge of Higher Worlds?
CW 11	From the Akasha-Chronicle
CW 12	Levels of Higher Knowledge
CW 13	Occult Science in Outline
CW 14	*Four Modern Mystery Dramas*
CW 15	The Spiritual Guidance of the Individual and Humanity
CW 16/17	*A Way of Self-Knowledge & The Threshold of the Spiritual World*
CW 18	The Riddles of Philosophy in Their History, Presented as an Outline
CW 18a	Views of the World and of Life in the Nineteenth Century
CW 19	Thoughts during the Time of War (1915) and Further Texts on the Events of the World War (1917–1921)
CW 20	The Riddles of the Human Being: Articulated and Unarticulated in the Thinking, Views and Opinions of a Series of German and Austrian Personalities
CW 21	The Riddles of the Soul
CW 22	Goethe's Spiritual Nature and Its Revelation in "Faust" and through the "Fairy Tale of the Snake and the Lily"
CW 23	The Central Points of the Social Question in the Necessities of Life in the Present and the Future
CW 24	Essays Concerning the Threefold Division of the Social Organism and the Period 1915–1921
CW 25	Three Steps of Anthroposophy. Philosophy – Cosmology – Religion
CW 26	Anthroposophical Leading Thoughts
CW 27	Fundamentals for Expansion of the Art of Healing according to Spiritual-Scientific Insights
CW 28	*Autobiography: Chapters in the Course of My Life: 1861–1907*

II. Collected Essays

CW 29	Collected Essays on Dramaturgy, 1889–1900
CW 30	Methodical Foundations of Anthroposophy: Collected Essays on Philosophy, Natural Science, Aesthetics and Psychology, 1884–1901
CW 31	Collected Essays on Culture and Current Events, 1887–1901
CW 32	Collected Essays on Literature, 1884–1902
CW 33	Biographies and Biographical Sketches, 1894–1905

CW 34 Lucifer-Gnosis: Foundational Essays on Anthroposophy and Reports from the Periodicals "Luzifer" and "Lucifer-Gnosis," 1903–1908
CW 35 Philosophy and Anthroposophy: Collected Essays, 1904–1923
CW 36 The Goetheanum-Idea in the Middle of the Cultural Crisis of the Present: Collected Essays from the Periodical "Das Goetheanum," 1921–1925
CW 37 Writings on the History of the Anthroposophical Movement and Society 1902–1925

III. Publications from the Literary Estate

CW 38/1 Complete Letters, Vol. 1: Weimar Period 1879–1890
CW 38/2 Complete Letters, Vol. 2: Weimar Period 1890–1897
CW 38/3 Complete Letters, Vol. 3: Early Berlin Period 1897–1905 [forthcoming]
CW 38/4 Complete Letters, Vol. 4: Activity within the Theosophical Society 1905–1912 [forthcoming]
CW 38/5 Complete Letters, Vol. 5: From the Founding of the Anthroposophical Society to the Opening of the Goetheanum 1913–1920 [forthcoming]
CW 38/6 Compelte Letters, Vol. 6: The Last Years 1920–1925 [forthcoming]
CW 40 Truth-Wrought Words
CW 40a Sayings, Poems and Mantras; Supplementary Volume
CW 41a Translations and Free Renderings from the Old and New Testaments
CW 41b Translations and Free Renderings of Various Works
CW 42 Stage Adaptations I: Dramas by Edouard Schuré
CW 43 Stage Adaptations II: The Oberufer Christmas Plays
CW 44 Sketches, Fragments and Paralipomena on the Four Mystery Dramas
CW 45 Anthroposophy: A Fragment from the Year 1910
CW 46 Posthumous Essays and Fragments 1879–1924
CW 47/48 Notebooks and Notepads (digital edition)
CW 49 Notes for and about Helmuth and Eliza von Moltke and Relatives, 1904–1924 [forthcoming]
CW 50 [Blank number]

B. Lectures

I. Public Lectures

CW 51 *On Philosophy, History, and Literature: Lectures at the Worker Education School and the Independent College, Berlin, 1901–1905*
CW 52 Spiritual Teachings Concerning the Soul and Observation of the World

CW 53	The Origin and Goal of the Human Being
CW 54	The Riddles of the World and Anthroposophy
CW 55	Knowledge of the Supersensible in Our Times and Its Meaning for Life Today
CW 56	Knowledge of the Soul and of the Spirit
CW 57	Where and How Does One Find the Spirit?
CW 58	The Metamorphoses of the Soul Life. Paths of Soul Experiences: Part One
CW 59	The Metamorphoses of the Soul Life. Paths of Soul Experiences: Part Two
CW 60	The Answers of Spiritual Science to the Biggest Questions of Existence
CW 61	Human History in the Light of Spiritual Research
CW 62	*Results of Spiritual Research*
CW 63	Spiritual Science as a Treasure for Life
CW 64	Out of Destiny-Burdened Times
CW 65	Out of Central European Spiritual Life
CW 66	Spirit and Matter, Life and Death
CW 67	The Eternal in the Human Soul. Immortality and Freedom
CW 68a	On the Being of Christianity
CW 68b	The Cycle of the Human Being within the Sense-, Soul-, and Spirit-World
CW 68c	Goethe and the Present
CW 68d	The Being of Man in the Light of Spiritual Science
CW 69a	Truths and Errors of Spiritual Research. Spiritual Science and the Future of Mankind
CW 69b	Knowledge and Immortality
CW 69c	New Christ-Experience
CW 69d	Death and Immortality in the Light of Spiritual Science
CW 69e	Spiritual Science and the Spiritual Goals of Our Time
CW 70a	Human Soul, Destiny and Death
CW 70b	Paths to the Knowledge of the Eternal Powers of the Human Soul
CW 71a	Soul Immortality [forthcoming]
CW 71b	The Human Being as a Soul and Spirit Being
CW 72	Freedom – Immortality – Social Life
CW 73	The Supplementing of the Modern Sciences through Anthroposophy
CW 73a	Specialized Fields of Knowledge and Anthroposophy
CW 74	The Philosophy of Thomas Aquinas
CW 75	*Anthroposophy and the Natural Sciences: Foundations and Methods*
CW 76	The Fructifying Effect of Anthroposophy on Specialized Fields
CW 77a	The Task of Anthroposophy in Relation to Science and Life: The Darmstadt College Course
CW 77b	Art and Anthroposophy. The Goetheanum-Impulse

CW 78 Anthroposophy, Its Roots of Knowledge and Fruits for Life
CW 79 The Reality of the Higher Worlds
CW 80a The Being of Anthroposophy
CW 80b The Inner Realm of Nature and the Being of the Human Soul
CW 80c Anthroposophical Spiritual Science and the Great Civilizational Questions of the Present
CW 81 *Reimagining Academic Studies: Science, Philosophy, Education, Social Science, Theology, Theory of Language*
CW 82 *Becoming Fully Human: The Significance of Anthroposophy in Contemporary Spiritual Life*
CW 83 *The Tension between East and West*
CW 84 *The Aims of Anthroposophy and the Purpose of the Goetheanum*
CW 85 Supplementary Volume: Individual Public Lectures I [forthcoming]
CW 86 Supplementary Volume: Individual Public Lectures II [forthcoming]

II. Lectures to the Members of the Anthroposophical Society

CW 87 Ancient Mysteries and Christianity
CW 88 *Concerning the Astral World and Devachan*
CW 89 Consciousness–Life–Form. Fundamental Principles of a Spiritual-Scientific Cosmology
CW 90a Self-knowledge and Knowledge of the Divine, Vol. I. Theosophy, Christology, and Mythology
CW 90b Self-knowledge and Knowledge of the Divine, Vol. II. Theosophy, Christology, and Mythology
CW 90c Theosophy and Occultism
CW 91 Cosmology and Human Evolution. Introduction to Theosophy – Theory of Colours
CW 92 *The Occult Truths of Myths and Legends: Greek and Germanic Mythology: Richard Wagner in the Light of Spiritual Science*
CW 93 The Temple Legend and the Golden Legend as a Symbolic Expression of Past and Future Secrets of Human Development. From the Contents of the Esoteric School
CW 93a Fundamentals of Esotericism
CW 94 Cosmogony. Popular Occultism. The Gospel of John. Theosophy Based on the Gospel of John

The Theosophy in the Gospel of John

CW 95 *Founding a Science of the Spirit*
CW 96 Origin-Impulses of Spiritual Science. Christian Esotericism in the Light of New Spirit-knowledge

CW 97	The Christian Mystery
CW 98	*Nature Beings and Spirit Beings: Their Activity in Our Visible World*
CW 99	*Rosicrucian Wisdom*
CW 100	*True Knowledge of the Christ: Theosophy and Rosicucianism—The Gospel of John*
CW 101	Myths and Legends. Occult Signs and Symbols
CW 102	*Good and Evil Spirits and Their Influence on Humanity*
CW 103	*The Gospel of John*
CW 104	The Apocalypse of John
CW 104a	From the Picture-Script of the Apocalypse of John
CW 105	*Universe, Earth, Human Being: Their Relationship to Egyptian Myths and Modern Civilization*
CW 106	Egyptian Myths and Mysteries in Relation to the Active Spiritual Forces of the Present
CW 107	*Disease, Karma, and Healing: Spiritual-scientific Enquiries into the Nature of the Human Being*
CW 108	Answering the Questions of Life and the World through Anthroposophy
CW 109	The Principle of Spiritual Economy in Connection with the Question of Reincarnation. An Aspect of the Spiritual Guidance of Humanity
CW 110	*The Spiritual Hierarchies and the Physical World: Zodiac, Planets, and Cosmos*
CW 111	Introduction to the Foundations of Theosophy
CW 112	The Gospel of John in Relation to the Three Other Gospels, Especially the Gospel of Luke
CW 113	The Orient in the Light of the Occident. The Children of Lucifer and the Brothers of Christ
CW 114	The Gospel of Luke
CW 115	Anthroposophy – Psychosophy – Pneumatosophy
CW 116	*The Christ-Impulse and the Development of Ego-Consciousness*
CW 117	*Deeper Secrets of Human Evolution in Light of the Gospels*
CW 117a	*The Gospel of John and the Three Other Gospels*
CW 118	The Event of the Christ-Appearance in the Etheric World
CW 119	*Macrocosm and Microcosm: The Greater and the Lesser World: Questions Concerning the Soul, Life and the Spirit*
CW 120	The Revelations of Karma
CW 121	*The Mission of Folk Souls*
CW 122	The Secrets of the Biblical Creation-Story. The Six-Day Work in the First Book of Moses
CW 123	The Gospel of Matthew
CW 124	*Background to the Gospel of St Mark*
CW 125	*Paths and Goals of the Spiritual Human Being: Life Questions in the Light of Spiritual Science*

CW 126 Occult History. Esoteric Observations of the Karmic Relationships of Personalities and Events of World History
CW 127 *The Mission of the New Spiritual Revelation: The Pivotal Nature of the Christ Event in Earth Evolution*
CW 128 An Occult Physiology
CW 129 *Wonders of the World: Trials of the Soul, Revelations of the Spirit*
CW 130 Esoteric Christianity and the Spiritual Guidance of Humanity
CW 131 *From Jesus to Christ*
CW 132 *Inner Experiences of Evolution*
CW 133 The Earthly and the Cosmic Human Being
CW 134 *The World of the Senses and the World of the Spirit*
CW 135 Reincarnation and Karma and Their Meaning for the Culture of the Present
CW 136 *Spiritual Beings in the Heavenly Bodies and in the Kingdoms of Nature*
CW 137 The Human Being in the Light of Occultism, Theosophy and Philosophy
CW 138 On Initiation. On Eternity and the Passing Moment. On the Light of the Spirit and the Darkness of Life
CW 139 The Gospel of Mark
CW 140 Occult Investigation into the Life between Death and New Birth. The Living Interaction between Life and Death
CW 141 *Between Death and Rebirth: In Relation to Cosmic Facts*
CW 142/46 *The Bhagavad Gita and the West: The Esoteric Significance of the Bhagavad Gita and Its Relation to the Epistles of Paul*
CW 143 *Three Paths to Christ: Experiencing the Supersensible*
CW 144 *The Mysteries of Initiation: From Isis to the Holy Grail*
CW 145 What Significance Does Occult Development of the Human Being Have for the Sheaths–Physical Body, Etheric Body, Astral Body, and Self?
CW 146 [See CW 142/46]
CW 147 The Secrets of the Threshold
CW 148 The Fifth Gospel
CW 149 *Christ and the Spiritual World: The Quest for the Holy Grail*
CW 150 *How the Spiritual World Projects into Physical Existence: The Influence of the Dead*
CW 151 *Human and Cosmic Thought*
CW 152 *Approaching the Mystery of Golgotha*
CW 153 The Inner Being of Man and Life Between Death and New Birth
CW 154 How does One Gain an Understanding of the Spiritual World? The Flowing in of Spiritual Impulses from out of the World of the Deceased
CW 155 *Christ and the Human Soul: The Meaning of Life – The Spiritual Foundation of Morality – Anthroposophy and Christianity*

CW 156 *Inner Reading and Inner Hearing: And How to Achieve Existence in the World of Ideas*
CW 157 *The Destinies of Individuals and Nations*
CW 157a The Formation of Destiny and the Life after Death
CW 158 *Our Connection with the Elemental World: Kalevala – Olaf Åsteson – the Russian People: The World as the Result of Balancing Influences*
CW 159 *The Mystery of Death: The Nature and Significance of Central Europe and the European Folk-Spirits*
CW 160 [Blank number]
CW 161 *Artistic Sensitivity as a Spiritual Approach to Knowing Life and the World*
CW 162 Questions of Art and Life in Light of Spiritual Science
CW 163 Coincidence, Necessity and Providence. Imaginative Knowledge and the Processes after Death
CW 164 *The Value of Thinking for a Cognition that Satisfies the Human Being: The Relationship between Spiritual Science and Natural Science*
CW 165 *Unifying Humanity Spiritually through the Christ Impulse*
CW 166 *Necessity and Freedom*
CW 167 *The Human Spirit Past and Present: Occult Fraternities and the Mystery of Golgotha*
CW 168 *The Connection between the Living and the Dead*
CW 169 World-being and Selfhood
CW 170 *The Riddle of Humanity*
CW 171 Inner Development-Impulses of Humanity. Goethe and the Crisis of the 19th Century.
CW 172 The Karma of the Vocation of the Human Being in Connection with Goethe's Life
CW 173a Observations of Modern History, Vol. I: Paths to an Objective Judgment
CW 173b Observations of Modern History, Vol. II: The Karma of Untruthfulness
CW 173c Observations of Modern History, Vol. III: The Reality of Occult Impulses
CW 174a *Europe Between East and West in Cosmic and Human History*
CW 174b *The Spiritual Background to the First World War*
CW 175 *Building Stones for an Understanding of the Mystery of Golgotha: Human Life in a Cosmic Context*
CW 176 *The Karma of Materialism: Aspects of Human Evolution*
CW 177 *The Fall of the Spirits of Darkness: The Spiritual Background to the Outer World: Spiritual Beings and Their Effects*
CW 178 Individual Spiritual Beings and Their Influence in the Soul of the Human Being

CW 179	*The Influence of the Dead on Destiny*
CW 180	Mystery Truths and Christmas Impulses. Ancient Myths and their Meaning
CW 181	*Dying Earth and Living Cosmos: The Living Gifts of Anthroposophy: The Need for New Forms of Consciousness*
CW 182	Death as Transformation of Life
CW 183	*Human Evolution: A Spiritual-Scientific Quest*
CW 184	*Eternal and Transient Elements in Human Life: The Cosmic Past of Humanity and the Mystery of Evil*
CW 185	Historical Symptomology
CW 185a	Historical-Developmental Foundations for Forming a Social Judgment
CW 186	The Fundamental Social Demands of Our Time. In Changed Times
CW 187	How Can Humanity Find the Christ Again? The Threefold Shadow-Existence of our Time and the New Christ-Light
CW 188	*Goetheanism, an Impulse of Transformation and Resurrection*
CW 189	*Conscious Society: Anthroposophy and the Social Question*
CW 190	*Past and Future Impulses in Societal Events*
CW 191	*Understanding Society through Spiritual-Scientific Knowledge: Social Threefolding, Christ, Lucifer, and Ahriman*
CW 192	Spiritual-Scientific Treatment of Social and Pedagogical Questions
CW 193	*Problems of Society: An Esoteric View, from Luciferic Past to Ahrimanic Future*
CW 194	*Michael's Mission: Revealing the Essential Secrets of Human Nature*
CW 195	*Cosmic New Year: Thoughts for New Year 1920*
CW 196	*What Is Necessary in These Urgent Times*
CW 197	*Polarities in the Evolution of Humanity: West and East – Materialism and Mysticism – Knowledge and Belief*
CW 198	*Healing the Social Organism*
CW 199	Spiritual Science as Knowledge of the Foundational Impulses of Social Formation
CW 200	The New Spirituality and the Christ-Experience of the 20th Century
CW 201	The Correspondences Between Microcosm and Macrocosm. The Human Being – A Hieroglyph of the Universe
CW 202	*Universal Spirituality and Human Physicality: Bridging the Divide: The Search for the New Isis and the Divine Sophia*
CW 203	The Responsibility of Human Beings for the Development of the World through their Spiritual Connection with the Planet Earth and the World of the Stars

CW 204 Perspectives of the Development of Humanity. The Materialistic Knowledge-Impulse and the Task of Anthroposophy
CW 205 *The Human Being as Body and Soul in Relation to the Cosmos*
CW 206 *The Human Being as Spiritual Being Evolving through the Course of History*
CW 207 Anthroposophy as Cosmosophy. Part One: Characteristic Features of the Human Being in the Earthly and the Cosmic Realms
CW 208 Anthroposophy as Cosmosophy. Part Two: The Forming of the Human Being as the Result of Cosmic Influence
CW 209 *The Language of the Cosmos: Cosmic Influences and the Spiritual Task of Northern Europe*
CW 210 *Old and New Methods of Initiation*
CW 211 *The Sun Mystery and the Mystery of Death and Resurrection: Exoteric and Esoteric Christianity*
CW 212 *Life of the Human Soul: And Its Relation to World Evolution*
CW 213 *Human Questions and Cosmic Answers*
CW 214 The Mystery of the Trinity: The Human Being in Relationship with the Spiritual World in the Course of Time
CW 215 Philosophy, Cosmology, and Religion in Anthroposophy
CW 216 *Supersensible Impulses in the Historical Development of Humanity*
CW 217 *Becoming the Archangel Michael's Companions: Rudolf Steiner's Challenge to the Younger Generation*
CW 217a *Youth and the Etheric Heart: Rudolf Steiner Speaks to the Younger Generation*
CW 218 *Spirit as Sculptor of the Human Organism*
CW 219 The Relationship of the World of the Stars to the Human Being, and of the Human Being to the World of the Stars. The Spiritual Communion of Humanity
CW 220 *Awake! For the Sake of the Future*
CW 221 Earth-Knowing and Heaven-Insight
CW 222 *The Driving Force of Spiritual Powers in World History*
CW 223 The Cycle of the Year as Breathing Process of the Earth and the Four Great Festival-Seasons. Anthroposophy and the Human Heart (*Gemüt*)
CW 224 The Human Soul and its Connection with Divine-Spiritual Individualities. The Internalization of the Festivals of the Year
CW 225 *Three Perspectives of Anthroposophy: Cultural Phenomena from the Point of View of Spiritual Science*
CW 226 Human Being, Human Destiny, and World Development
CW 227 Initiation-Knowledge
CW 228 *Initiation Science: And the Development of the Human Mind*

CW 229	The Experiencing of the Course of the Year in Four Cosmic Imaginations
CW 230	The Human Being as Harmony of the Creative, Building, and Formative World-Word
CW 231	The Supersensible Human Being, Understood Anthroposophically
CW 232	The Forming of the Mysteries
CW 233	*World History and the Mysteries in the Light of Anthroposophy*
CW 233a	*Rosicrucianism and Modern Initiation: Mystery Centres of the Middle Ages: The Easter Festival and the History of the Mysteries*
CW 234	Anthroposophy. A Summary after 21 Years
CW 235	Esoteric Observations of Karmic Relationships in 6 Volumes, Vol. 1
CW 236	Esoteric Observations of Karmic Relationships in 6 Volumes, Vol. 2
CW 237	Esoteric Observations of Karmic Relationships in 6 Volumes, Vol. 3: The Karmic Relationships of the Anthroposophical Movement
CW 238	Esoteric Observations of Karmic Relationships in 6 Volumes, Vol. 4: The Spiritual Life of the Present in Relationship to the Anthroposophical Movement
CW 239	Esoteric Observations of Karmic Relationships in 6 Volumes, Vol. 5
CW 240	Esoteric Observations of Karmic Relationships in 6 Volumes, Vol. 6
CW 241	[Blank number]
CW 242	[Blank number]
CW 243	*True and False Paths of Spiritual Research*
CW 244	Answers to Questions, and Interviews
CW 245	[Blank number]
CW 246	Supplementary Volume I: Individual Members Lectures
CW 247	Supplementary Volume II: Individual Members Lectures
CW 248	[Blank number]
CW 249	[Blank number]
CW 250	On the History of the German Section of the Theosophical Society 1902–1913. Lectures, Speeches, Reports, and Minutes
CW 251	On the History of the Anthroposophical Society 1913–1922
CW 252	On the History of the Building Association and the Goetheanum Association 1911–1924
CW 253	*Sexuality, Inner Development, and Community Life: Ethical and Spiritual Dimensions of the Crisis in the Anthroposophical Society in Dornach, 1915*

CW 254 The Occult Movement in the 19th Century and Its Relationship to World Culture. Significant Points from the Exoteric Cultural Life around the Middle of the 19th Century
CW 255b Anthroposophy and Its Opponents
CW 256 [Blank number]
CW 257 Anthroposophical Community-Building
CW 258 *The Anthroposophic Movement: The History and Conditions of the Anthroposophical Movement in Relation to the Anthroposophical Society: An Encouragement for Self-Examination*
CW 259 The Year of Destiny 1923 in the History of the Anthroposophical Society. From the Burning of the Goetheanum to the Christmas Conference
CW 260 The Christmas Conference for the Founding of the General Anthroposophical Society 1923/24
CW 260a The Constitution of the General Anthroposophical Society and the School for Spiritual Science. The Rebuilding of the Goetheanum
CW 261 *Our Dead: Memorial, Funeral, and Cremation Addresses 1906–1924*
CW 262 Rudolf Steiner and Marie Steiner-von Sivers: Correspondence and Documents, 1901–1925
CW 263/1 Rudolf Steiner and Edith Maryon: Correspondence: Letters, Verses, Sketches, 1912–1924
CW 264 *From the History and Contents of the First Section of the Esoteric School: Letters, Documents, and Lectures: 1904–1914*
CW 265 *Freemasonry and Ritual Work: The Misraim Service*
CW 265a Teaching and Instruction Lessons for Members of the Knowledge-Cultic Section of the Esoteric School 1904–1914 [forthcoming]
CW 266/1 *From the Esoteric School: Esoteric Lessons 1904–1909*
CW 266/2 *From the Esoteric School: Esoteric Lessons 1910–1912*
CW 266/3 *From the Esoteric School: Esoteric Lessons 1913–1923*
CW 267 *Soul Exercises: Word and Symbol Meditations*
CW 268 *Mantric Sayings: Meditations 1903–1925*
CW 269 Ritual Texts for the Celebration of the Free Christian Religious Instruction. The Collected Verses for Teachers and Students of the Waldorf School
CW 270 Esoteric Instructions for the First Class of the School for Spiritual Science at the Goetheanum 1924, 4 Volumes

III. Lectures and Courses on Specific Realms of Life Lectures on Art

CW 271 *Art and Theory of Art: Foundations of a New Aesthetics*
CW 272 *Anthroposophy in the Light of Goethe's* Faust*: Volume One of Spiritual-Scientific Commentaries on Goethe's* Faust

CW 273 *Goethe's* Faust *in the Light of Anthroposophy: Volume Two of Spiritual-Scientific Commentaries on Goethe's* Faust
CW 274 Addresses for the Christmas Plays from the Old Folk Traditions
CW 275 Art in the Light of Mystery Wisdom
CW 276 *The Arts and Their Mission*
CW 277a The Origin and Development of Eurythmy 1912–1918
CW 277b The Origin and Development of Eurythmy 1918–1920
CW 277c The Origin and Development of Eurythmy 1920–1922 [forthcoming]
CW 277d The Origin and Development of Eurythmy 1923–1924 [forthcoming]
CW 278 Eurythmy as Visible Song
CW 279 *Eurythmy as Speech Made Visible: Speech Eurythmy Course*
CW 280 The Method and Nature of Speech Formation
CW 281 The Art of Recitation and Declamation
CW 282 Speech Formation and Dramatic Art
CW 283 *The Inner Nature of Music and the Experience of Tone*
CW 284 *Rosicrucianism Renewed: The Unity of Art, Science & Religion: The Theosophical Congress of Whitsun 1907*
CW 285 [Blank number]
CW 286 Paths to a New Style of Architecture. "And the Building Becomes Man"
CW 287 *Architecture as Peacework: The First Goetheanum, Dornach, 1914*
CW 288 *Architecture, Sculpture, and Painting of the First Goetheanum*
CW 289 The Building-Idea of the Goetheanum: Lectures with Slides from the Years 1920–1921
CW 290 *Toward a New Theory of Architecture: The First Goetheanum in Pictures [no longer in the German GA]*
CW 291 The Being of Colours
CW 291a Knowledge of Colours. Supplementary Volume to "The Being of Colours"
CW 292 *Art History as a Reflection of Inner Spiritual Impulses*

Lectures on Education

CW 293 General Knowledge of the Human Being as the Foundation of Pedagogy
CW 294 The Art of Education: Methodology and Didactics
CW 295 The Art of Education: Seminar Discussions and Lectures on Lesson Planning
CW 296 The Question of Education as a Social Question
CW 297 The Idea and Practice of the Waldorf School

CW 297a	Education for Life: Self-Education and the Practice of Pedagogy
CW 298	Rudolf Steiner in the Waldorf School
CW 299	Spiritual-Scientific Observations on Speech
CW 300a	Conferences with the Teachers of the Free Waldorf School in Stuttgart, 1919 to 1924, in 3 Volumes, Vol. 1
CW 300b	Conferences with the Teachers of the Free Waldorf School in Stuttgart, 1919 to 1924, in 3 Volumes, Vol. 2
CW 300c	Conferences with the Teachers of the Free Waldorf School in Stuttgart, 1919 to 1924, in 3 Volumes, Vol. 3
CW 301	The Renewal of Pedagogical-Didactical Art through Spiritual Science
CW 302	Knowledge of the Human Being and the Forming of Class Lessons
CW 302a	Education and Teaching from a Knowledge of the Human Being
CW 303	The Healthy Development of the Human Being
CW 304	Methods of Education and Teaching Based on Anthroposophy
CW 304a	Anthroposophical Knowledge of the Human Being and Pedagogy
CW 305	The Soul-Spiritual Foundational Forces of the Art of Education. Spiritual Values in Education and Social Life
CW 306	Pedagogical Praxis from the Viewpoint of a Spiritual-Scientific Knowledge of the Human Being. The Education of the Child and Young Human Beings
CW 307	The Spiritual Life of the Present and Education
CW 308	The Method of Teaching and the Life-Requirements for Teaching
CW 309	Anthroposophical Pedagogy and Its Prerequisites
CW 310	The Pedagogical Value of a Knowledge of the Human Being and the Cultural Value of Pedagogy
CW 311	The Art of Education from an Understanding of the Being of Humanity

Lectures on Medicine

CW 312	*Introducing Anthroposophical Medicine*
CW 313	*Illness and Therapy: Spiritual-Scientific Aspects of Healing*
CW 314	*Physiology and Healing: Treatment, Therapy, and Hygiene*
CW 315	Curative Eurythmy
CW 316	*Understanding Healing: Meditative Reflections on Deepening Medicine through Spiritual Science*
CW 317	*Education for Special Needs: The Curative Education Course*
CW 318	The Working Together of Doctors and Pastors
CW 319	*The Healing Process: Spirit, Nature & Our Bodies*

Lectures on Natural Science

CW 320 Spiritual-Scientific Impulses for the Development of Physics 1: The First Natural-Scientific Course: Light, Colour, Tone, Mass, Electricity, Magnetism
CW 321 Spiritual-Scientific Impulses for the Development of Physics 2: The Second Natural-Scientific Course: Warmth at the Border of Positive and Negative Materiality
CW 322 The Borders of the Knowledge of Nature
CW 323 *Interdisciplinary Astronomy: Third Scientific Course*
CW 324 Nature Observation, Mathematics, and Scientific Experimentation and Results from the Viewpoint of Anthroposophy
CW 324a The Fourth Dimension in Mathematics and Reality
CW 325 Natural Science and the World-Historical Development of Humanity since Ancient Times
CW 326 The Moment of the Coming Into Being of Natural Science in World History and Its Development Since Then
CW 327 *Agriculture: Spiritual-Scientific Foundations for Agricultural Renewal*

Lectures on Social Life and the Threefold Arrangement of the Social Organism

CW 328 *The Social Challenge*
CW 329 The Liberation of the Human Being as the Foundation for a New Social Form
CW 330 The Renewal of the Social Organism
CW 331 Work-Council and Socialization
CW 332a The Social Future
CW 332b Lectures and Speeches on Social and Economic Issues
CW 333 *Freedom of Thought and Societal Forces: Implementing the Demands of Modern Society*
CW 334 From the Unified State to the Threefold Social Organism
CW 335 The Crisis of the Present and the Path to Healthy Thinking
CW 336 The Great Questions of the Times and Anthroposophical Spiritual Knowledge
CW 337a Social Ideas, Social Realities, Social Practice, Vol. 1: Question-and-Answer Evenings and Study Evenings of the Alliance for the Threefold Social Organism in Stuttgart, 1919–1920
CW 337b Social Ideas, Social Realities, Social Practice, Vol. 2: Discussion Evenings of the Swiss Alliance for the Threefold Social Organism

CW 338 *Communicating Anthroposophy: The Course for Speakers to Promote the Idea of Threefolding*

CW 339 Anthroposophy, Threefold Social Organism, and the Art of Public Speaking

CW 340/41 *Rethinking Economics: Lectures and Seminars on World Economics*

Lectures and Courses on Christian Religious Work

CW 342 *First Steps in Christian Religious Renewal: Preparing the Ground for The Christian Community*

CW 343 Lectures and Courses on Christian Religious Work, Vol. 2: Spiritual Knowledge – Religious Feeling – Cultic Doing

CW 344 Lectures and Courses on Christian Religious Work, Vol. 3: Lectures at the Founding of The Christian Community

CW 345 Lectures and Courses on Christian Religious Work, Vol. 4: Concerning the Nature of the Working Word

CW 346 Lectures and Courses on Christian Religious Work, Vol. 5: The Apocalypse and the Work of the Priest

Lectures for Workers at the Goetheanum

CW 347 The Knowledge of the Nature of the Human Being According to Body, Soul and Spirit. On Earlier Conditions of the Earth

CW 348 On Health and Illness. Foundations of a Spiritual-Scientific Doctrine of the Senses

CW 349 On the Life of the Human Being and of the Earth. On the Nature of Christianity

CW 350 Rhythms in the Cosmos and in the Human Being. How Does One Come To See the Spiritual World?

CW 351 The Human Being and the World. The Influence of the Spirit in Nature. On the Nature of Bees

CW 352 Nature and the Human Being Observed Spiritual-Scientifically

CW 353 The History of Humanity and the World-Views of the Folk Cultures

CW 354 The Creation of the World and the Human Being. Life on Earth and the Influence of the Stars

C. Artistic Works

CW A 1–10; 57 The Architectural Work I: The Goetheanum and Its Predecessors

CW A 11 The Sculptural Work

CW A 12 The Goetheanum Windows. The Speech of Light. Sketches and Studies

CW A 13–16;
52–56 Painting Work
CW A 14 Sketches for the Painting of the Small Dome of the First Goetheanum
CW A 27–43 The Architectural Work II: Commercial and Residential Buildings in Dornach and Other Places [forthcoming]
CW A 45 The Graphic Work
CW A 48 The Drawing Work
CW A 51 The Art of Jewellry as a Goethean Language of Form
CW A 54.0 A Path of Training in Painting. Pastel Sketches and Watercolours
CW A 54.1 Nature Moods. Nine Training Sketches for Painters

Eurythmy Figures

CW A 26 Skectches of the Eurythmy Figures
CW A 26a The Eurythmy Figures of Rudolf Steiner, Artistically Executed by Annemarie Bäschlin
CW A 26b Eurythmy Figures from the Time When They Were Created

Eurythmy Forms

CW A 23/1 Volume I: Eurythmy Forms for Poems by Rudolf Steiner
CW A 23/2 Volume II: Eurythmy Forms for the Calendar of the Soul by Rudolf Steiner
CW A 23/3 Volume III: Euythmy Forms for Poems by J. W. von Goethe
CW A 23/4 Volume IV: Eurythmy Forms for Poems by Christian Morgenstern
CW A 23/5 Volume V: Eurythmy Forms for Poems by Albert Steffen
CW A 23/6 Volume VI: Eurythmy Forms for German Poems by Fercher von Steinwand, Hamerling, Hebbel, C. F. Meyer, Nietzsche, among others
CW A 23/7 Volume VII: Eurythmy Forms for English Poems
CW A 23/8 Volume VIII: Eurythmy Forms for French and Russian Poems
CW A 24 Volume IX: Eurythmy Forms for Tone Eurythmy

Blackboard Drawings from Lectures

CW A 58/1 Volume I: 20 Plates from Public Lectures 1920–1924 in CWs 73a, 74, 76, and 84
CW A 58/2 Volume II: 38 Plates from Lectures in 1919 in CWs 191 and 194
CW A 58/3 Volume III: 34 Plates from Lectures in 1920 in CWs 196 and 198
CW A 58/4 Volume IV: 33 Plates from Lectures in 1920 in CWs 199 and 200
CW A 58/5 Volume V: 31 Plates from Lectures in 1920 in CW 201
CW A 58/6 Volume VI: 46 Plates from Lectures 1920–1921 in CWs 202–204

CW A 58/7 Volume VII: 38 Plates from Lectures in 1921 in CWs 205 and 206
CW A 58/8 Volume VIII: 42 Plates from Lectures in 1921 in CWs 207–209
CW A 58/9 Volume IX: 40 Plates from Lectures in 1922 in CWs 210–212
CW A 58/10 Volume X: 35 Plates from Lectures in 1922 in CWs 213–215
CW A 58/11 Volume XI: 41 Plates from Lectures 1922–1923 in CWs 216, 218–220
CW A 58/12 Volume XII: 37 Plates from Lectures in 1923 in CWs 221–225
CW A 58/13 Volume XIII: 38 Plates from Lectures in 1923 in CWs 227–230
CW A 58/14 Volume XIV: 36 Plates from Lectures in 1923 in CWs 232 and 233
CW A 58/15 Volume XV: 37 Plates from Lectures in 1924 in CWs 233a, 234, and 243
CW A 58/16 Volume XVI: 56 Plates from the "Karma Lectures" in CWs 235–238 and 240
CW A 58/17 Volume XVII: 21 Plates from Lectures on the History of the Anthroposophical Society in CWs 257, 258, 260, and 260a
CW A 58/18 Volume XVIII: 33 Plates from Lectures on Art in CWs 271, 276, 283, 288–290, and 291
CW A 58/19 Volume XIX: 41 Plates from Lectures on Eurythmy in CWs 278, 279, and 315
CW A 58/20 Volume XX: 27 Plates from Lectures on Speech Formation in CWs 281 and 282
CW A 58/21 Volume XXI: 42 Plates from Lectures on Education in CWs 296, 303, 304, 306, and 311
CW A 58/22 Volume XXII: 46 Plates from Lectures on Medicine in CWs 312–315
CW A 58/23 Volume XXIII: 48 Plates from Lectures in 1924 in CWs 316–318
CW A 58/24 Volume XXIV: 39 Plates from Lectures on Natural Science and the Social Question in CWs 322, 326, 327, 339, and 340
CW A 58/25 Volume XXV: 33 Plates from the "Workers Lectures" (Volumes 1 and 2) in CWs 347 and 348
CW A 58/26 Volume XXVI: 51 Plates from the "Workers Lectures" (Volumes 3 and 4) in CWs 349 and 350
CW A 58/27 Volume XXVII: 35 Plates from the "Workers Lectures" (Volumes 5 and 6) in CWs 351 and 352
CW A 58/28 Volume XXVIII: 42 Plates from the "Workers Lectures" (Volumes 7 and 8) in CWs 353 and 354
CW A 58/29 Volume XXIX: 43 Plates from Lectures and Courses on Christian Religious Activity in CWs 342–344 and 346
CW A 58/30 Volume XXX: 27 Plates from CWs 255b, 324a, 337b, and 340, Corrigenda, Plates without CW Assignment, Copies

SIGNIFICANT EVENTS IN THE LIFE OF RUDOLF STEINER

1829: June 23: birth of Johann Steiner (1829–1910)—Rudolf Steiner's father—in Geras, Lower Austria.

1834: May 8: birth of Franciska Blie (1834–1918)—Rudolf Steiner's mother—in Horn, Lower Austria. 'My father and mother were both children of the glorious Lower Austrian forest district north of the Danube.'

1860: May 16: marriage of Johann Steiner and Franciska Blie.

1861: February 25: birth of *Rudolf Joseph Lorenz Steiner* in Kraljevec, Croatia, near the border with Hungary, where Johann Steiner works as a telegrapher for the South Austria Railroad. Rudolf Steiner is baptized two days later, February 27, the date usually given as his birthday.

1862: Summer: the family moves to Mödling, Lower Austria.

1863: The family moves to Pottschach, Lower Austria, near the Styrian border, where Johann Steiner becomes stationmaster. 'The view stretched to the mountains . . . majestic peaks in the distance and the sweet charm of nature in the immediate surroundings.'

1864: November 15: birth of Rudolf Steiner's sister, Leopoldine (d. November 1, 1927). She will become a seamstress and live with her parents for the rest of her life.

1866: July 28: birth of Rudolf Steiner's deaf-mute brother, Gustav (d. May 1, 1941).

1867: Rudolf Steiner enters the village school. Following a disagreement between his father and the schoolmaster, whose wife falsely accused the boy of causing a commotion, Rudolf Steiner is taken out of school and taught at home.

1868: A critical experience. Unknown to the family, an aunt dies in a distant town. Sitting in the station waiting room, Rudolf Steiner sees her 'form', which speaks to him, asking for help. 'Beginning with this experience, a new soul life began in the boy, one in which not only the outer trees and mountains spoke to him, but also the worlds that lay behind them. From this moment on, the boy began to live with the spirits of nature . . .'

1869: The family moves to the peaceful, rural village of Neudorfl, near Wiener Neustadt in present-day Austria. Rudolf Steiner attends the village school. Because of the 'unorthodoxy' of his writing and spelling, he has to do 'extra lessons'.

1870: Through a book lent to him by his tutor, he discovers geometry: 'To grasp something purely in the spirit brought me inner happiness. I know that I first learned happiness through geometry.' The same tutor allows him to draw, while other students still struggle with their reading and writing. 'An artistic element' thus enters his education.

1871: Though his parents are not religious, Rudolf Steiner becomes a 'church child', a favourite of the priest, who was 'an exceptional character'. 'Up to the age of ten or eleven, among those I came to know, he was far and away the most significant.' Among other things, he introduces Steiner to Copernican, heliocentric cosmology. As an altar boy, Rudolf Steiner serves at Masses, funerals, and Corpus Christi processions. At year's end, after an incident in which he escapes a thrashing, his father forbids him to go to church.

1872: Rudolf Steiner transfers to grammar school in Wiener-Neustadt, a five-mile walk from home, which must be done in all weathers.

1873–75: Through his teachers and on his own, Rudolf Steiner has many wonderful experiences with science and mathematics. Outside school, he teaches himself analytic geometry, trigonometry, differential equations, and calculus.

1876: Rudolf Steiner begins tutoring other students. He learns bookbinding from his father. He also teaches himself stenography.

1877: Rudolf Steiner discovers Kant's *Critique of Pure Reason,* which he reads and rereads. He also discovers and reads von Rotteck's *World History.*

1878: He studies extensively in contemporary psychology and philosophy.

1879: Rudolf Steiner graduates from high school with honours. His father is transferred to Inzersdorf, near Vienna. He uses his first visit to Vienna 'to purchase a great number of philosophy books'—Kant, Fichte, Schelling, and Hegel, as well as numerous histories of philosophy. His aim: to find a path from the 'I' to nature.

October 1879–1883: Rudolf Steiner attends the Technical College in Vienna—to study mathematics, chemistry, physics, mineralogy, botany, zoology, biology, geology, and mechanics—with a scholarship. He also attends lectures in history and literature, while avidly reading philosophy on his own. His two favourite professors are Karl Julius Schröer (German language and literature) and Edmund Reitlinger (physics). He also audits lectures by Robert Zimmermann on aesthetics and Franz Brentano on philosophy. During this year he begins his friendship with Moritz Zitter (1861–1921), who will help support him financially when he is in Berlin.

1880: Rudolf Steiner attends lectures on Schiller and Goethe by Karl Julius Schröer, who becomes his mentor. Also 'through a remarkable combination of circumstances', he meets Felix Koguzki, a 'herb gatherer' and healer, who could 'see deeply into the secrets of nature'. Rudolf Steiner will meet and study with this 'emissary of the Master' throughout his time in Vienna.

1881: January: '... I didn't sleep a wink. I was busy with philosophical problems until about 12:30 a.m. Then, finally, I threw myself down on my couch. All my striving during the previous year had been to research whether the following statement by Schelling was true or not: *Within everyone dwells a secret, marvellous capacity to draw back from the stream of time—out of the self clothed in all that comes to us from outside—into our innermost being and there, in the immutable form of the Eternal, to look into ourselves.* I believe, and I am still quite certain of it, that I discovered this capacity in myself; I had long had an inkling of it. Now the whole of idealist philosophy stood before me in modified form. What's a sleepless night compared to that!'

Rudolf Steiner begins communicating with leading thinkers of the day, who send him books in return, which he reads eagerly.

July: 'I am not one of those who dives into the day like an animal in human form. I pursue a quite specific goal, an idealistic aim—knowledge of the truth! This cannot be done offhandedly. It requires the greatest striving in the world, free of all egotism, and equally of all resignation.'

August: Steiner puts down on paper for the first time thoughts for a 'Philosophy of Freedom'. 'The striving for the absolute: this human yearning is freedom.' He also seeks to outline a 'peasant philosophy', describing what the worldview of a 'peasant'—one who lives close to the earth and the old ways—really is.

1881–1882: Felix Koguzki, the herb gatherer, reveals himself to be the envoy of another, higher initiatory personality, who instructs Rudolf Steiner to penetrate Fichte's philosophy and to master modern scientific thinking as a preparation for right entry into the spirit. This 'Master' also teaches him the double (evolutionary and involutionary) nature of time.

1882: Through the offices of Karl Julius Schröer, Rudolf Steiner is asked by Joseph Kürschner to edit Goethe's scientific works for the *Deutsche National-Literatur* edition. He writes 'A Possible Critique of Atomistic Concepts' and sends it to Friedrich Theodor Vischer.

1883: Rudolf Steiner completes his college studies and begins work on the Goethe project.

1884: First volume of Goethe's *Scientific Writings* (CW 1) appears (March). He lectures on Goethe and Lessing, and Goethe's approach to science. In July, he enters the household of Ladislaus and Pauline Specht as tutor to the four Specht boys. He will live there until 1890. At this time, he meets Josef Breuer (1842–1925), the co-author with Sigmund Freud of *Studies in Hysteria,* who is the Specht family doctor.

1885: While continuing to edit Goethe's writings, Rudolf Steiner reads deeply in contemporary philosophy (Eduard von Hartmann, Johannes Volkelt, and Richard Wahle, among others).

1886: May: Rudolf Steiner sends Kürschner the manuscript of *Outlines of Goethe's Theory of Knowledge* (CW 2), which appears in October, and which he sends out widely. He also meets the poet Marie Eugenie Delle Grazie and writes 'Nature and Our Ideals' for her. He attends her salon, where he meets many priests, theologians, and philosophers, who will become his friends. Meanwhile, the director of the Goethe Archive in Weimar requests his collaboration with the *Sophien* edition of Goethe's works, particularly the writings on colour.

1887: At the beginning of the year, Rudolf Steiner is very sick. As the year progresses and his health improves, he becomes increasingly 'a man of letters', lecturing, writing essays, and taking part in Austrian cultural life. In August–September, the second volume of Goethe's *Scientific Writings* appears.

1888: January–July: Rudolf Steiner assumes editorship of the 'German Weekly' *(Deutsche Wochenschrift*). He begins lecturing more intensively, giving, for example, a lecture titled 'Goethe as Father of a New Aesthetics'. He meets and becomes soul friends with Friedrich Eckstein (1861–1939), a vegetarian, philosopher of symbolism, alchemist, and musician, who will introduce him to various spiritual currents (including Theosophy) and with whom he will meditate and interpret esoteric and alchemical texts.

1889: Rudolf Steiner first reads Nietzsche *(Beyond Good and Evil).* He encounters Theosophy again and learns of Madame Blavatsky in the theosophical circle around Marie Lang (1858–1934). Here he also meets well-known figures of Austrian life, as well as esoteric figures like the occultist Franz Hartmann and Karl Leinigen-Billigen (translator of C.G. Harrison's *The Transcendental Universe)*. During this period, Steiner first reads A.P. Sinnett's *Esoteric Buddhism* and Mabel Collins's *Light on the Path*. He also begins travelling, visiting Budapest, Weimar, and Berlin (where he meets philosopher Eduard von Hartmann).

1890: Rudolf Steiner finishes Volume 3 of Goethe's scientific writings. He begins his doctoral dissertation, which will become *Truth and Science* (CW 3). He also meets the poet and feminist Rosa Mayreder (1858–1938), with whom he can exchange his most intimate thoughts. In September, Rudolf Steiner moves to Weimar to work in the Goethe-Schiller Archive.

1891: Volume 3 of the Kürschner edition of Goethe appears. Meanwhile, Rudolf Steiner edits Goethe's studies in mineralogy and scientific writings for the *Sophien* edition. He meets Ludwig Laistner of the Cotta Publishing Company, who asks for a book on the basic question of metaphysics. From this will result, ultimately, *The Philosophy of Freedom* (CW 4), which will be published not by Cotta but by Emil Felber. In October, Rudolf Steiner takes the oral exam for a doctorate in philosophy, mathematics, and mechanics at Rostock University, receiving his doctorate on the twenty-sixth. In November, he gives his first lecture on Goethe's 'Fairy Tale' in Vienna.

1892: Rudolf Steiner continues work at the Goethe-Schiller Archive and on his *Philosophy of Freedom*. *Truth and Science,* his doctoral dissertation, is published. Steiner undertakes to write Introductions to books on Schopenhauer and Jean Paul for Cotta. At year's end, he finds lodging with Anna Eunike, née Schulz (1853–1911), a widow with four daughters and a son. He also develops a friendship with Otto Erich Hartleben (1864–1905) with whom he shares literary interests.

1893: Rudolf Steiner begins his habit of producing many reviews and articles. In March, he gives a lecture titled 'Hypnotism, with Reference to Spiritism'. In September, volume 4 of the Kürschner edition is completed. In November, *The Philosophy of Freedom* appears. This year, too, he meets John Henry Mackay (1864–1933), the anarchist, and Max Stirner, a scholar and biographer.

1894: Rudolf Steiner meets Elisabeth Fürster Nietzsche, the philosopher's sister, and begins to read Nietzsche in earnest, beginning with the as yet unpublished *Antichrist.* He also meets Ernst Haeckel (1834–1919). In the fall, he begins to write *Nietzsche, A Fighter against His Time* (CW 5).

1895: May, *Nietzsche, A Fighter against His Time* appears.

1896: January 22: Rudolf Steiner sees Friedrich Nietzsche for the first and only time. Moves between the Nietzsche and the Goethe-Schiller

Archives, where he completes his work before year's end. He falls out with Elisabeth Förster Nietzsche, thus ending his association with the Nietzsche Archive.

1897: Rudolf Steiner finishes the manuscript of *Goethe's Worldview* (CW 6). He moves to Berlin with Anna Eunike and begins editorship of the *Magazin für Literatur*. From now on, Steiner will write countless reviews, literary and philosophical articles, and so on. He begins lecturing at the 'Free Literary Society'. In September, he attends the Zionist Congress in Basel. He sides with Dreyfus in the Dreyfus affair.

1898: Rudolf Steiner is very active as an editor in the political, artistic, and theatrical life of Berlin. He becomes friendly with John Henry Mackay and poet Ludwig Jacobowski (1868–1900). He joins Jacobowski's circle of writers, artists, and scientists—'The Coming Ones' (*Die Kommenden)*—and contributes lectures to the group until 1903. He also lectures at the 'League for College Pedagogy'. He writes an article for Goethe's sesquicentennial, 'Goethe's Secret Revelation', on the 'Fairy Tale of the Green Snake and the Beautiful Lily'.

1898–99: 'This was a trying time for my soul as I looked at Christianity. . . . I was able to progress only by contemplating, by means of spiritual perception, the evolution of Christianity. . . . Conscious knowledge of real Christianity began to dawn in me around the turn of the century. This seed continued to develop. My soul trial occurred shortly before the beginning of the twentieth century. It was decisive for my soul's development that I stood spiritually before the Mystery of Golgotha in a deep and solemn celebration of knowledge.'

1899: Rudolf Steiner begins teaching and giving lectures and lecture cycles at the Workers' College, founded by Wilhelm Liebknecht (1826–1900). He will continue to do so until 1904. Writes: *Literature and Spiritual Life in the Nineteenth Century; Individualism in Philosophy; Haeckel and His Opponents; Poetry in the Present;* and begins what will become (fifteen years later) *The Riddles of Philosophy* (CW 18). He also meets many artists and writers, including Käthe Kollwitz, Stefan Zweig, and Rainer Maria Rilke. On October 31, he marries Anna Eunike.

1900: 'I thought that the turn of the century must bring humanity a new light. It seemed to me that the separation of human thinking and willing from the spirit had peaked. A turn or reversal of direction in human evolution seemed to me a necessity.' Rudolf Steiner finishes *World and Life Views in the Nineteenth Century* (the second part of what will become *The Riddles of Philosophy)* and dedicates it to

Ernst Haeckel. It is published in March. He continues lecturing at *Die Kommenden,* whose leadership he assumes after the death of Jacobowski. Also, he gives the Gutenberg Jubilee lecture before 7,000 typesetters and printers. In September, Rudolf Steiner is invited by Count and Countess Brockdorff to lecture in the Theosophical Library. His first lecture is on Nietzsche. His second lecture is titled 'Goethe's Secret Revelation.' October 6, he begins a lecture cycle on the mystics that will become *Mystics after Modernism* (CW 7). November–December: 'Marie von Sivers appears in the audience. . . .' Also in November, Steiner gives his first lecture at the Giordano Bruno Bund (where he will continue to lecture until May, 1905). He speaks on Bruno and modern Rome, focusing on the importance of the philosophy of Thomas Aquinas as monism.

1901: In continual financial straits, Rudolf Steiner's early friends Moritz Zitter and Rosa Mayreder help support him. In October, he begins the lecture cycle *Christianity as Mystical Fact* (CW 8) at the Theosophical Library. In November, he gives his first 'theosophical lecture' on Goethe's 'Fairy Tale' in Hamburg at the invitation of Wilhelm Hubbe-Schleiden. He also attends a gathering to celebrate the founding of the Theosophical Society at Count and Countess Brockdorff's. He gives a lecture cycle, 'From Buddha to Christ,' for the circle of the *Kommenden.* November 17, Marie von Sivers asks Rudolf Steiner if Theosophy needs a Western–Christian spiritual movement (to complement Theosophy's Eastern emphasis). 'The question was posed. Now, following spiritual laws, I could begin to give an answer. . . .' In December, Rudolf Steiner writes his first article for a theosophical publication. At year's end, the Brockdorffs and possibly Wilhelm Hubbe-Schleiden ask Rudolf Steiner to join the Theosophical Society and undertake the leadership of the German section. Rudolf Steiner agrees, on the condition that Marie von Sivers (then in Italy) work with him.

1902: Beginning in January, Rudolf Steiner attends the opening of the Workers' School in Spandau with Rosa Luxemberg (1870–1919). January 17, Rudolf Steiner joins the Theosophical Society. In April, he is asked to become general secretary of the German Section of the Theosophical Society, and works on preparations for its founding. In July, he visits London for a theosophical congress. He meets Bertram Keightly, G.R.S. Mead, A.P. Sinnett, and Annie Besant, among others. In September, *Christianity as Mystical Fact* appears. In October, Rudolf Steiner gives his first public lecture on Theosophy ('Monism and Theosophy') to about three hundred people at the Giordano Bruno Bund. On October 19–21, the

German Section of the Theosophical Society has its first meeting; Rudolf Steiner is the general secretary, and Annie Besant attends. Steiner lectures on practical karma studies. On October 23, Annie Besant inducts Rudolf Steiner into the Esoteric School of the Theosophical Society. On October 25, Steiner begins a weekly series of lectures: 'The Field of Theosophy'. During this year, Rudolf Steiner also first meets Ita Wegman (1876–1943), who will become his close collaborator in his final years.

1903: Rudolf Steiner holds about 300 lectures and seminars. In May, the first issue of the periodical *Luzifer* appears. In June, Rudolf Steiner visits London for the first meeting of the Federation of the European Sections of the Theosophical Society, where he meets Colonel Olcott. He begins to write *Theosophy* (CW 9).

1904: Rudolf Steiner continues lecturing at the Workers' College and elsewhere (about 90 lectures), while lecturing intensively all over Germany among theosophists (about 140 lectures). In February, he meets Carl Unger (1878–1929), who will become a member of the board of the Anthroposophical Society (1913). In March, he meets Michael Bauer (1871–1929), a Christian mystic, who will also be on the board. In May, *Theosophy* appears, with the dedication: 'To the spirit of Giordano Bruno'. Rudolf Steiner and Marie von Sivers visit London for meetings with Annie Besant. June: Rudolf Steiner and Marie von Sivers attend the meeting of the Federation of European Sections of the Theosophical Society in Amsterdam. In July, Steiner begins the articles in *Luzifer-Gnosis* that will become *How to Know Higher Worlds* (CW 10) and *Cosmic Memory* (CW 11). In September, Annie Besant visits Germany. In December, Steiner lectures on Freemasonry. He mentions the High Grade Masonry derived from John Yarker and represented by Theodore Reuss and Karl Kellner as a blank slate 'into which a good image could be placed'.

1905: This year, Steiner ends his non-theosophical lecturing activity. Supported by Marie von Sivers, his theosophical lecturing—both in public and in the Theosophical Society—increases significantly: 'The German Theosophical Movement is of exceptional importance.' Steiner recommends reading, among others, Fichte, Jacob Boehme, and Angelus Silesius. He begins to introduce Christian themes into Theosophy. He also begins to work with doctors (Felix Peipers and Ludwig Noll). In July, he is in London for the Federation of European Sections, where he attends a lecture by Annie Besant: 'I have seldom seen Mrs Besant speak in so inward and heartfelt a manner... Through Mrs Besant I have found the way to H.P. Blavatsky.' September to October, he gives a course of 31 lectures for a small group of esoteric students. In October, the annual meeting of the German Section of the Theosophical Society, which still remains very small, takes place. Rudolf Steiner reports membership has risen from 121 to 377 members. In November, seeking to establish esoteric 'continuity', Rudolf Steiner and Marie von Sivers participate in a 'Memphis-Misraim' Masonic ceremony. They pay 45 marks for membership. 'Yesterday, you saw how little remains of former esoteric institutions.' 'We are dealing only with a "framework" ... for the present, nothing lies behind it. The occult powers have completely withdrawn.'

1906: Expansion of theosophical work. Rudolf Steiner gives about 245 lectures, only 44 of which take place in Berlin. Cycles are given in Paris, Leipzig, Stuttgart, and Munich. Esoteric work also intensifies. Rudolf Steiner begins writing *An Outline of Esoteric Science* (CW 13). In January, Rudolf Steiner receives permission (a patent) from the Great Orient of the Scottish A & A Thirty-Three Degree Rite of the Order of the Ancient Freemasons of the Memphis-Misraim Rite to direct a chapter under the name 'Mystica Aeterna.' This will become the 'Cognitive-Ritual Section' (also called 'Misraim Service') of the Esoteric School. (See: *Freemasonry and Ritual Work: The Misraim Service,* CW 265.) During this time, Steiner also meets Albert Schweitzer. In May, he is in Paris, where he visits Édouard Schuré. Many Russians attend his lectures (including Konstantin Balmont, Dimitri Mereszkovski, Zinaida Hippius, and Maximilian Woloshin). He attends the General Meeting of the European Federation of the Theosophical Society, at which Col Olcott is present for the last time. He spends the year's end in Venice and Rome, where he writes and works on his translation of H.P. Blavatsky's *Key to Theosophy.*

1907: Further expansion of the German Theosophical Movement according to the Rosicrucian directive to 'introduce spirit into the world'—in education, in social questions, in art, and in science. In February, Col Olcott dies in Adyar. Before he dies, Olcott indicates that 'the Masters' wish Annie Besant to succeed him: much politicking ensues. Rudolf Steiner supports Besant's candidacy. April–May: preparations for the Congress of the Federation of European Sections of the Theosophical Society—the great, watershed Whitsun 'Munich Congress,' attended by Annie Besant and others. Steiner decides to separate Eastern and Western (Christian–Rosicrucian) esoteric schools. He takes his esoteric school out of the Theosophical Society (Besant and Rudolf Steiner are 'in harmony' on this). Steiner makes his first lecture tours to Austria and

Hungary. That summer, he is in Italy. In September, he visits Édouard Schuré, who will write the Introduction to the French edition of *Christianity as Mystical Fact* in Barr, Alsace. Rudolf Steiner writes the autobiographical statement known as the 'Barr Document.' In *Luzifer-Gnosis*, 'The Education of the Child' appears.

1908: The movement grows (membership: 1,150). Lecturing expands. Steiner makes his first extended lecture tour to Holland and Scandinavia, as well as visits to Naples and Sicily. Themes: St John's Gospel, the Apocalypse, Egypt, science, philosophy, and logic. *Luzifer-Gnosis* ceases publication. In Berlin, Marie von Sivers (with Johanna Mücke (1864–1949) forms the *Philosophisch-Theosophisch* (after 1915 *Philosophisch-Anthroposophisch) Verlag* to publish Steiner's work. Steiner gives lecture cycles titled *The Gospel of St John* (CW 103) and *The Apocalypse* (104).

1909: *An Outline of Esoteric Science* appears. Lecturing and travel continues. Rudolf Steiner's spiritual research expands to include the polarity of Lucifer and Ahriman; the work of great individualities in history; the Maitreya Buddha and the Bodhisattvas; spiritual economy (CW 109); the work of the spiritual hierarchies in heaven and on earth (CW 110). He also deepens and intensifies his research into the Gospels, giving lectures on the Gospel of St Luke (CW 114) with the first mention of two Jesus children. Meets and becomes friends with Christian Morgenstern (1871–1914). In April, he lays the foundation stone for the Malsch model—the building that will lead to the first Goetheanum. In May, the International Congress of the Federation of European Sections of the Theosophical Society takes place in Budapest. Rudolf Steiner receives the Subba Row medal for *How to Know Higher Worlds*. During this time, Charles W. Leadbeater discovers Jiddu Krishnamurti (1895–1986) and proclaims him the future 'world teacher,' the bearer of the Maitreya Buddha and the 'reappearing Christ.' In October, Steiner delivers seminal lectures on 'anthroposophy,' which he will try, unsuccessfully, to rework over the next years into the unfinished work, *Anthroposophy (A Fragment)* (CW 45).

1910: New themes: *The Reappearance of Christ in the Etheric* (CW 118); *The Fifth Gospel; The Mission of Folk Souls* (CW 121); *Occult History* (CW 126); the evolving development of etheric cognitive capacities. Rudolf Steiner continues his Gospel research with *The Gospel of St Matthew* (CW 123). In January, his father dies. In April, he takes a month-long trip to Italy, including Rome, Monte Cassino, and Sicily. He also visits Scandinavia again. July–August, he writes the first Mystery Drama, *The Portal of Initiation* (CW 14). In November, he gives 'psychosophy' lectures. In December, he submits 'On the

Psychological Foundations and Epistemological Framework of Theosophy' to the International Philosophical Congress in Bologna.

1911: The crisis in the Theosophical Society deepens. In January, 'The Order of the Rising Sun,' which will soon become 'The Order of the Star in the East,' is founded for the coming world teacher, Krishnamurti. At the same time, Marie von Sivers, Rudolf Steiner's co-worker, falls ill. Fewer lectures are given, but important new ground is broken. In Prague, in March, Steiner meets Franz Kafka (1883–1924) and Hugo Bergmann (1883–1975). In April, he delivers his paper to the Philosophical Congress. He writes the second Mystery Drama, *The Soul's Probation* (CW 14). Also, while Marie von Sivers is convalescing, Rudolf Steiner begins work on *Calendar 1912/1913*, which will contain the 'Calendar of the Soul' meditations. On March 19, Anna (Eunike) Steiner dies. In September, Rudolf Steiner visits Einsiedeln, birthplace of Paracelsus. In December, Friedrich Rittelmeyer, future founder of The Christian Community, meets Rudolf Steiner. The *Johannes-Bauverein,* the 'building committee,' which would lead to the first Goetheanum (first planned for Munich), is also founded, and a preliminary committee for the founding of an independent association is created that, in the following year, will become the Anthroposophical Society. Important lecture cycles include *Occult Physiology* (CW 128); *Wonders of the World* (CW 129); *From Jesus to Christ* (CW 131). Other themes: esoteric Christianity; Christian Rosenkreutz; the spiritual guidance of humanity; the sense world and the world of the spirit.

1912: Despite the ongoing, now increasing crisis in the Theosophical Society, much is accomplished: *Calendar 1912/1913* is published; eurythmy is created; both the third Mystery Drama, *The Guardian of the Threshold* (CW 14) and *A Way of Self-Knowledge* (CW 16) are written. New (or renewed) themes included life between death and rebirth and karma and reincarnation. Other lecture cycles: *Spiritual Beings in the Heavenly Bodies and in the Kingdoms of Nature* (CW 136); *The Human Being in the Light of Occultism, Theosophy, and Philosophy* (CW 137); *The Gospel of St Mark* (CW 139); and *The Bhagavad Gita and the Epistles of Paul* (CW 142). On May 8, Rudolf Steiner celebrates White Lotus Day, H.P. Blavatsky's death day, which he had faithfully observed for the past decade, for the last time. In August, Rudolf Steiner suggests the 'independent association' be called the 'Anthroposophical Society.' In September, the first eurythmy course takes place. In October, Rudolf Steiner declines recognition of a Theosophical Society lodge dedicated to the Star of the East and decides to expel all Theosophical Society members belonging to the order.

Also, with Marie von Sivers, he first visits Dornach, near Basel, Switzerland, and they stand on the hill where the Goetheanum will be built. In November, a Theosophical Society lodge is opened by direct mandate from Adyar (Annie Besant). In December, a meeting of the German section occurs at which it is decided that belonging to the Order of the Star of the East is incompatible with membership in the Theosophical Society. December 28: informal founding of the Anthroposophical Society in Berlin.

1913: Expulsion of the German section from the Theosophical Society. February 2–3: Foundation meeting of the Anthroposophical Society. Board members include: Marie von Sivers, Michael Bauer, and Carl Unger. September 20: Laying of the foundation stone for the *Johannes Bau* (Goetheanum) in Dornach. Building begins immediately. The fourth Mystery Drama, *The Soul's Awakening* (CW 14), is completed. Also: *The Threshold of the Spiritual World* (CW 147). Lecture cycles include: *The Bhagavad Gita and the Epistles of Paul* and *The Esoteric Meaning of the Bhagavad Gita* (CW 146), which the Russian philosopher Nikolai Berdyaev attends; *The Mysteries of the East and of Christianity* (CW 144); *The Effects of Esoteric Development* (CW 145); and *The Fifth Gospel* (CW 148). In May, Rudolf Steiner is in London and Paris, where anthroposophical work continues.

1914: Building continues on the *Johannes Bau* (Goetheanum) in Dornach, with artists and co-workers from seventeen nations. The general assembly of the Anthroposophical Society takes place. In May, Rudolf Steiner visits Paris, as well as Chartres Cathedral. June 28: assassination in Sarajevo ('Now the catastrophe has happened!'). August 1: War is declared. Rudolf Steiner returns to Germany from Dornach—he will travel back and forth. He writes the last chapter of *The Riddles of Philosophy*. Lecture cycles include: *Human and Cosmic Thought* (CW 151); *Inner Being of Humanity between Death and a New Birth* (CW 153); *Occult Reading and Occult Hearing* (CW 156). December 24: marriage of Rudolf Steiner and Marie von Sivers.

1915: Building continues. Life after death becomes a major theme, also art. Writes: *Thoughts during a Time of War* (CW 24). Lectures include: *The Secret of Death* (CW 159); *The Uniting of Humanity through the Christ Impulse* (CW 165).

1916: Rudolf Steiner begins work with Edith Maryon (1872–1924) on the sculpture 'The Representative of Humanity' ('The Group'—Christ, Lucifer, and Ahriman). He also works with the alchemist Alexander von Bernus on the quarterly *Das Reich*. He writes *The Riddle of Humanity* (CW 20). Lectures include: *Necessity and Freedom in World History and Human Action* (CW 166); *Past and Present in the*

Human Spirit (CW 167); *The Karma of Vocation* (CW 172); *The Karma of Untruthfulness* (CW 173).

1917: Russian Revolution. The U.S. enters the war. Building continues. Rudolf Steiner delineates the idea of the 'threefold nature of the human being' (in a public lecture March 15) and the 'threefold nature of the social organism' (hammered out in May–June with the help of Otto von Lerchenfeld and Ludwig Polzer-Hoditz in the form of two documents titled *Memoranda,* which were distributed in high places). August–September: Rudolf Steiner writes *The Riddles of the Soul* (CW 20). Also: commentary on 'The Chymical Wedding of Christian Rosenkreutz' for Alexander Bernus (Das *Reich*). Lectures include: *The Karma of Materialism* (CW 176); *The Spiritual Background of the Outer World: The Fall of the Spirits of Darkness* (CW 177).

1918: March 18: peace treaty of Brest-Litovsk—'Now everything will truly enter chaos! What is needed is cultural renewal.' June: Rudolf Steiner visits Karlstein (Grail) Castle outside Prague. Lecture cycle: *From Symptom to Reality in Modern History* (CW 185). In mid-November, Emil Molt, of the Waldorf-Astoria Cigarette Company, has the idea of founding a school for his workers' children.

1919: Focus on the threefold social organism: tireless travel, countless lectures, meetings, and publications. At the same time, a new public stage of Anthroposophy emerges as cultural renewal begins. The coming years will see initiatives in pedagogy, medicine, pharmacology, and agriculture. January 27: threefold meeting: 'We must first of all, with the money we have, found free schools that can bring people what they need.' February: first public eurythmy performance in Zurich. Also: 'Appeal to the German People' (CW 24), circulated March 6 as a newspaper insert. In April, *Towards Social Renewal* (CW 23) appears—'perhaps the most widely read of all books on politics appearing since the war'. Rudolf Steiner is asked to undertake the 'direction and leadership' of the school founded by the Waldorf-Astoria Company. Rudolf Steiner begins to talk about the 'renewal' of education. May 30: a building is selected and purchased for the future Waldorf School. August–September, Rudolf Steiner gives a lecture course for Waldorf teachers, *The Foundations of Human Experience (Study of Man)* (CW 293). September 7: Opening of the first Waldorf School. December (into January): first science course, the *Light Course* (CW 320).

1920: The Waldorf School flourishes. New threefold initiatives. Founding of limited companies *Der Kommende Tag* and *Futurum A.G.* to infuse spiritual values into the economic realm. Rudolf Steiner also focuses on the sciences. Lectures: *Introducing Anthroposophical*

Medicine (CW 312); *The Warmth Course* (CW 321); *The Boundaries of Natural Science* (CW 322); *The Redemption of Thinking* (CW 74). February: Johannes Werner Klein—later a co-founder of The Christian Community—asks Rudolf Steiner about the possibility of a 'religious renewal,' a 'Johannine church.' In March, Rudolf Steiner gives the first course for doctors and medical students. In April, a divinity student asks Rudolf Steiner a second time about the possibility of religious renewal. September 27–October 16: anthroposophical 'university course.' December: lectures titled *The Search for the New Isis* (CW 202).

1921: Rudolf Steiner continues his intensive work on cultural renewal, including the uphill battle for the threefold social order. 'University' arts, scientific, theological, and medical courses include: *The Astronomy Course* (CW 323); *Observation, Mathematics, and Scientific Experiment* (CW 324); the *Second Medical Course* (CW 313); *Colour*. In June and September–October, Rudolf Steiner also gives the first two 'priests' courses' (CW 342 and 343). The 'youth movement' gains momentum. Magazines are founded: *Die Drei* (January), and—under the editorship of Albert Steffen (1884–1963)—the weekly, *Das Goetheanum* (August). In February–March, Rudolf Steiner takes his first trip outside Germany since the war (Holland). On April 7, Steiner receives a letter regarding 'religious renewal,' and May 22–23, he agrees to address the question in a practical way. In June, the Klinical-Therapeutic Institute opens in Arlesheim under the direction of Dr Ita Wegman. In August, the Chemical-Pharmaceutical Laboratory opens in Arlesheim (Oskar Schmiedel and Ita Wegman are directors). The Clinical Therapeutic Institute is inaugurated in Stuttgart (Dr Ludwig Noll is director); also the Research Laboratory in Dornach (Ehrenfried Pfeiffer and Gunther Wachsmuth are directors). In November–December, Rudolf Steiner visits Norway.

1922: The first half of the year involves very active public lecturing (thousands attend); in the second half, Rudolf Steiner begins to withdraw and turn toward the Society—'The Society is asleep.' It is 'too weak' to do what is asked of it. The businesses—*Der Kommende Tag* and *Futurum A.G.*—fail. In January, with the help of an agent, Steiner undertakes a twelve-city German lecture tour, accompanied by eurythmy performances. In two weeks he speaks to more than 2,000 people. In April, he gives a 'university course' in The Hague. He also visits England. In June, he is in Vienna for the East–West Congress. In August–September, he is back in England for the Oxford Conference on Education. Returning to Dornach, he gives the lectures *Philosophy, Cosmology, and*

Religion (CW 215), and gives the third priests' course (CW 344). On September 16, The Christian Community is founded. In October–November, Steiner is in Holland and England. He also speaks to the youth: *The Youth Course* (CW 217). In December, Steiner gives lectures titled *The Origins of Natural Science* (CW 326), and *Humanity and the World of Stars: The Spiritual Communion of Humanity* (CW 219). December 31: Fire at the Goetheanum, which is destroyed.

1923: Despite the fire, Rudolf Steiner continues his work unabated. A very hard year. Internal dispersion, dissension, and apathy abound. There is conflict—between old and new visions—within the Society. A wake-up call is needed, and Rudolf Steiner responds with renewed lecturing vitality. His focus: the spiritual context of human life; initiation science; the course of the year; and community building. As a foundation for an artistic school, he creates a series of pastel sketches. Lecture cycles: *The Anthroposophical Movement; Initiation Science* (CW 227) (in Wales at the Penmaenmawr Summer School); *The Four Seasons and the Archangels* (CW 229); *Harmony of the Creative Word* (CW 230); *The Supersensible Human* (CW 231), given in Holland for the founding of the Dutch Society. On November 10, in response to the failed Hitler-Ludendorff putsch in Munich, Steiner closes his Berlin residence and moves the *Philosophisch-Anthroposophisch Verlag* (Press) to Dornach. On December 9, Steiner begins the serialization of his *Autobiography: The Course of My Life* (CW 28) in *Das Goetheanum*. It will continue to appear weekly, without a break, until his death. Late December–early January: Rudolf Steiner re-founds the Anthroposophical Society (about 12,000 members internationally) and takes over its leadership. The new board members are: Marie Steiner, Ita Wegman, Albert Steffen, Elisabeth Vreede, and Gunther Wachsmuth. (See *The Christmas Meeting for the Founding of the General Anthroposophical Society,* CW 260.) Accompanying lectures: *Mystery Knowledge and Mystery Centres* (CW 232); *World History in the Light of Anthroposophy* (CW 233). December 25: the Foundation Stone is laid (in the hearts of members) in the form of the 'Foundation Stone Meditation.'

1924: January 1: having founded the Anthroposophical Society and taken over its leadership, Rudolf Steiner has the task of 'reforming' it. The process begins with a weekly newssheet ('What's Happening in the Anthroposophical Society') in which Rudolf Steiner's 'Letters to Members' and 'Anthroposophical Leading Thoughts' appear (CW 26). The next step is the creation of a new esoteric class, the 'first class' of the 'University of Spiritual Science' (which was to have been followed, had Rudolf Steiner lived longer, by two more advanced classes). Then comes a new language for

Anthroposophy—practical, phenomenological, and direct; and Rudolf Steiner creates the model for the second Goetheanum. He begins the series of extensive 'karma' lectures (CW 235–40); and finally, responding to needs, he creates two new initiatives: biodynamic agriculture and curative education. After the middle of the year, rumours begin to circulate regarding Steiner's health. Lectures: January–February, *Anthroposophy* (CW 234); February: *Tone Eurythmy* (CW 278); June: *The Agriculture Course* (CW 327); June–July: *Speech Eurythmy* (CW 279); *Curative Education* (CW 317); August: (England, 'Second International Summer School'), *Initiation Consciousness: True and False Paths in Spiritual Investigation* (CW 243); September: *Pastoral Medicine* (CW 318). On September 26, for the first time, Rudolf Steiner cancels a lecture. On September 28, he gives his last lecture. On September 29, he withdraws to his studio in the carpenter's shop; now he is definitively ill. Cared for by Ita Wegman, he continues working, however, and writing the weekly instalments of his *Autobiography* and *Letters to the Members/Leading Thoughts* (CW 26).

1925: Rudolf Steiner, while continuing to work, continues to weaken. He finishes *Extending Practical Medicine* (CW 27) with Ita Wegman. On March 30, around ten in the morning, Rudolf Steiner dies.

Index

Steiner

A NOTE FROM RUDOLF STEINER PRESS

We are an independent publisher and registered charity (non-profit organisation) dedicated to making available the work of Rudolf Steiner in English translation. We care a great deal about the content of our books and have hundreds of titles available – as printed books, ebooks and in audio formats.

As a publisher devoted to anthroposophy...

- We continually commission translations of previously unpublished works by Rudolf Steiner and invest in re-translating, editing and improving our editions.
- We are committed to making anthroposophy available to all by publishing introductory books as well as contemporary research.
- Our new print editions and ebooks are carefully checked and proofread for accuracy, and converted into all formats for all platforms.
- Our translations are officially authorised by Rudolf Steiner's estate in Dornach, Switzerland, to whom we pay royalties on sales, thus assisting their critical work.

So, look out for Rudolf Steiner Press as a mark of quality and support us today by buying our books, or contact us should you wish to sponsor specific titles or to support the charity with a gift or legacy.

office@rudolfsteinerpress.com
Join our e-mailing list at www.rudolfsteinerpress.com

RUDOLF STEINER PRESS